XXX NAZi'k

FEAR, GREED AND THE END OF THE RAINBOW

Guarding Your Assets in the Coming Bear Market

FEAR, GREED AND THE END OF THE RAINBOW

ANDREW SARLOS
WITH PATRICIA BEST

KEY PORTER BOOKS

To my wife, Mary, whose love, support, and dedication have sustained me over the years, and most especially during these past few months.

1997

Canadian Cataloguing in Publication Data

Sarlos, Andrew
    Fear, greed and the end of the rainbow : guarding your assets in
    the coming bear market

ISBN 1-55013-896-0

1. Stocks. 2. Speculation. 3. Economic forecasting.
I. Best, Patricia. II. Title.

HG6041.S37   1997   332.63'22   C97-930964-6

The publisher gratefully acknowledges the support of the Canada Council for the Arts and the Ontario Arts Council for its publishing program.

Key Porter Books Limited
70 The Esplanade
Toronto, Ontario
Canada M5E 1R2

Printed and bound in Canada

97 98 99 00 6 5 4 3 2

Contents

Acknowledgements

The ideas contained in this book are entirely my own, but not all of the words are, and so I wish to thank Patricia Best for her writing and research contribution. My gratitude also to Peter DeSario, who was kind enough to spend a great deal of time reading and commenting on the manuscript. (Peter's bulletin, *Wave(s) of the Future(s)*, is available by calling [561] 283-9552.) Also, my thanks to Ian McAvity, who helped me, in the earliest stages of this project, in formulating my thesis. (Ian's newsletter, *Deliberations*, is available at P.O. Box 40097, Tucson, AZ 85717.) Paul Gottlieb also lent an important hand in the first research stages, for which I am grateful. Another friend whose commentaries and ideas I admire and find invaluable is Don Coxe, chairman of Harris Investment Management Inc., and I want to acknowledge his influence on this book. As well, his colleagues in the economics department of Nesbitt Burns Inc. are due my thanks for supplying numerous statistics, dates, and stock prices quickly and cheerfully.

In putting this book together, data and information came from many sources. Especially helpful were the following books: *A Short History of Financial Euphoria* by John Kenneth Galbraith; *Bear Markets: How to Survive and Make Money in Them* by Harry D. Schultz; *The Great Bull Market: Wall Street in the 1920s*, *The Last Bull Market: Wall Street in the 1960s*, and *Panic on Wall Street: A History of America's Financial Disasters*, all by Robert Sobel; *Market Volatility* by Robert J. Shiller; *Investment Fundamentals* by Roger W. Babson; *At the Crest of the Tidal Wave* by Robert Prechter, Jr.; and *Rebuilding Wall Street* by Mark Fadiman.

As well, certain newsletters and journals proved extremely valuable: *The Bank Credit Analyst*, Richard Russell's *Dow Theory Letters*, *The International Harry Schultz Letter*, *William's Inference Service* (Vol. 24, no. 1 [Winter 1976]), *The Journal of Economic History* (Vol. 50, no. 2 [June 1990]), and *Volatility and Panic in the Nation's Financial Markets* (U.S. Government Printing Office, November 4, 1987).

In addition, regular coverage of the markets and the economy in *The Globe & Mail* and *The Financial Post* provided a helpful ongoing tracking of events; as well I relied on *The Wall Street Journal*'s coverage of the Dow's 100th anniversary; certain articles in *Fortune, Forbes*, and *Euromoney*; and almost anything by Alan Abelson in *Barron's*.

Finally, my thanks to Beverley Slopen for her invaluable advice, to editor Bernice Eisenstein for her thoroughness, and to Anna Porter for her faith in this book.

Andrew Sarlos
April 1997

The Siren's Call

"Financial genius is a rising stock market."
—JOHN KENNETH GALBRAITH

"Never confuse a bull market and brains."
—WALL STREET AXIOM

O n a table in my office is a bronze casting of two beasts: a bull wrestling a bear to the ground. It is a copy of the famous tableau that stands outside the New York Stock Exchange. The bull's charge forward is an apt anthropomorphic representation of the drive and enthusiasm inherent in capitalism for growth, profit, and gain. One hears of "pawing-the-ground bullishness" and one thinks of a rush to riches. The bear, by contrast, is a negative symbol of hibernation, with his treacherous claws ready to harm anyone foolish enough to venture forward. Most investors today are familiar with only one of the pair of creatures that habitually roam the stock market. They have forgotten that the symbiosis of the market requires opposing forces locked in combat—the bull and the bear, the optimists and the pessimists, the buyers but also the sellers.

For fifteen years the bull has indeed wrestled the bear into submission. But I am convinced that the bear's time will come. This century began with a bear market, which started in December 1899 and hit bottom in June 1900, and it could very well end with one as well.

As I write this in late April 1997, North American stock markets have bounced back remarkably from a 10 per cent drop during March (the first official "correction" in seven years) after spending the early part of this year hitting record after record and surpassing the 7000 level. The Toronto Stock Exchange 300 index soared 26 per cent during 1996, and early this year moved beyond the 6300 level. Euphoria is abroad in the land. Ordinary folks are mad for stocks, convinced that their value has nowhere to go but up. Many people are getting rich on their investments, having enjoyed the longest bull market in history. A great many of them are making money in stocks *for the very first time*, and they are loving it. Maybe you are one. These investors have heeded the bull market's siren call, pulling their precious savings out of banks and ploughing them into mutual funds by the tens of billions of dollars each month.

After all, North Americans have taken seriously the warnings their governments have given them: that they had better start saving for their own retirements because the government pension may not be there for them when they reach age sixty-five. When they look around in this low-inflation world of today, they see GICs and CDs and Treasury bills paying only a few percentage points. That's not good enough for a comfortable retirement. Then they look at the bull market roaring away on the stock exchanges and they see gains of 20 per cent and 30 per cent, and even 60 per cent. They leap into the equity frenzy, lapping up emerging market funds, value funds, growth funds—almost any fund. They pat themselves on the back. They are savvy investors. Their nest eggs are growing splendidly.

This bull market was born at 776.92 points (using the Dow Jones Industrial Average as a measurement) in August 1982. At that point, investors were mired in a slough of despond, holding out little hope that enrichment would be found in the stock market. The vicious bear of the mid-1970s and the ravages of hyperinflation during that decade were uppermost in most investors' minds. Of course, at the darkest hour comes a new dawn, and since 1982 we have not seen a year in which the Dow low has broken below that of the preceding year—an amazing record, and an unprecedented string of rises. (The previous such string was for six years in the postwar boom of the 1940s.) In the past two years, in New York, the Dow has smashed through the 4000, 5000, 6000, and 7000 barriers. Since 1982, this bull has recorded a phenomenal 800 per cent gain. The famous Roaring '20s bull market, by contrast, achieved a 497 per cent return. The twenty-year bull running from the late 1940s to the late 1960s recorded a cumulative return of 406 per cent.

Unfortunately, the party we are currently enjoying is destined to come to a calamitous end very soon.

Mutual-fund mania has gripped North America during the 1990s. The exhortations from gurus and experts and salespeople is that stocks for the long term beat every other kind of investing. But I believe we are headed for a bear market of such severity that the personal savings of many North Americans will be wiped out at precisely the point in their lives when they can least readily withstand the loss.

I foresee a Dow of 3000. Some of you will be especially hard hit. Those who arrived late to the party in the last couple of years—and in Canada that is 45 per cent of all holders of equity mutual funds—will have bought high, and I predict you will sell low in the midst of a creeping panic that will move through Wall Street and Bay Street. Those who are fifty-plus years of age risk losing most of what you have built for your retirement, if you don't get out in time.

For thirty years, I have traded stocks on the major stock markets, making millions and losing plenty too. I have been a financier, playing a part in some of the major takeovers in the 1970s and 1980s in Canada; at times my personal trading has accounted for as much as 10 per cent of the daily volume on the Toronto Stock Exchange. My love of trading arises from my enjoyment of the challenge of pitting my intellect and my judgement of the moment against the conventional wisdom. I truly believe that the stock market is a barometer, not a thermometer, and as such reflects changes in market sentiment virtually before they are recognized.

Because of my success in the stock market, I am usually asked about ways to get rich. But, in the next few years, I predict that people will be asking me how they can avoid financial ruin.

I do not mean to be alarmist. And if you search the financial newspapers and magazines, you will not find this view expressed very often. Certainly, your broker won't tell you about the coming bear market; it's not in his or her best interest to do so. Your mutual fund salesperson won't tell you what happens to his or her 1-800 number when thousands of panicky investors call to pull out their money. In today's market, the mood is one of optimism, and even arrogance—as if the good times can go on for ever. This Time Is Different, say the bulls, meaning that the stock market and the economy in general have entered a "new paradigm" of low inflation, adept central banks, a global appetite for North American goods and services, and a finely honed productivity in our domestic industries. They mean that the various signals that the 1996–97 bull is overheated are irrelevant because the economic and corporate context has changed. The bulls would have you believe that a secular bear market is simply not possible anymore.

For some time I've been convinced that we are in the last stages of a speculative blow-off of this bull-market cycle. In February 1994, I put myself on the record in a speech to members of Ontario Hydro's Pension Investment Fund Committee. Ontario Hydro's pension fund puts $8 billion into the market, and I certainly got their attention when I called for an explosive surge in equity markets followed by a collapse of 30 to 50 per cent. At the time, I noted that stocks were trading at, near, or above all-time-high valuations, whether you measured them relative to earnings, dividends, or book value. I noted that the stock market continued to march ever higher despite pervasive pessimism, suspicion, and doubt about the economy. But I asked rhetorically, do bull markets end with careful, creeping-up action? Do bull markets end amid scepticism and warnings? The answer is yes: markets that continue to push relentlessly, but cautiously, higher generally end with explosive action, "blowing off" on the upside amid surprise and excitement.

I have learned to think of markets in terms of the unexpected. So, at the time of my speech, I asked myself: What would be the most unexpected thing this market could do? My answer was a major market surge to the upside—an explosion. And I was right. Since then the New

York market—and finally Toronto's—has been tracking skyward on a parabolic curve.

I know that what follows a parabolic curve is a decline to the beginning of the curve. Remember Newton's third law: each action is followed by an equal and opposite reaction. That law explains why all parabolic advances—and I will describe a few of them—are followed by collapses.

So why, when all the signs of a topping bull were there in 1995, has it lasted well into 1997? An unexpected development in liquidity levels in the United States flooded capital markets and has delayed what I still see as the inevitable. (I explore that more thoroughly in Chapter 2.) But the net effect of it was that it breathed fresh life into a bull market that has held on longer than anyone dared believe.

My forecast to the Ontario Hydro gathering recalled another fearless prediction of mine, made in September 1987. Maurice Strong, the former chairman of Petro-Canada and more recently Ontario Hydro, has been a friend of mine for many years. That September, Maurice had a group of friends and associates to his ranch in the Baca Valley in Colorado to talk about business, the economy, and the environment. Among those in attendance were Canadian and American business and political figures. I gave a presentation on the markets. Remember, this was the overheated summer of 1987, when people were buying into mutual funds at a frantic pace, and the Dow was headed straight up. I told the group gathered at Maurice's ranch that the market was headed for a major decline of as much as 1000 points and I said it could happen within one month, and certainly by the end of the year. You know the rest. The New York stock market, and subsequently every major stock exchange in the world, went into massive free-fall during a few heart-stopping days in late October 1987. It became known as the Crash of '87, echoing a similar market meltdown in 1929.

So today why do I believe that we are coming closer and closer to the moment when a major reversal must occur? There is the evidence of economic history. In the past five hundred years, up cycles lasting fifty or sixty years have been followed by down cycles of ten years or so. In the past fifty years, since the Second World War, the world economy has been on a growth binge. At least, that was the case until 1991, when for the first time the world's economy did not grow. We are due for a down cycle.

Then there is the behaviour of the market. Generally speaking, the greater the rise, the greater the fall, or, as the market analysts like to call it, "reversion to the mean," which is a fancy way of asking: How different from "normal" is the current situation? As an example, look at Japan's Nikkei index. The recent run-up on the Dow Jones Industrial Average and the Standard & Poor's 500 is strikingly similar to the steep curve of the Nikkei in the late 1980s. The party ended for the Tokyo market in December 1989, as the Nikkei went from a top of 38957, to 14194 in August 1992. Five years later, it has made something of a comeback to the 20000 level, but that is still far below its peak, and the prognosis for much more of a recovery is not all that good.

Predicting the market is a difficult thing. Obviously, anyone who could do it accurately and 100 per cent consistently would be the richest person on the planet. Most forecasters will predict only one thing: either the amount the market will rise or fall, or when it will happen. But there are no geniuses in the market. Sooner or later, you are wrong on something. I have no expectation that I will be right every time; I'm perfectly happy simply being right more often than I'm wrong. That is the only way you can expect to make money in the market as a professional stock trader. After all, professional baseball pays men millions of dollars to hit in one out of three at-bats.

There is the famous story of Roger Babson, a prominent economist in the early part of this century, declaring in September 1929 that "sooner or later a crash is coming, and it may be terrific." The trouble was, of course, that he had made similar, though not quite as dramatic, predictions in the previous few years. As a result, he was ridiculed and scorned in the early fall of 1929—at least, he was until the Great Crash began in October.

For investors, it is enough to see the general picture and act on it. That is what this book is about. Market timing has been pretty well discredited by many years of rising prices. And it has taken a lot of flack from "experts," especially those who want to sell you mutual funds to hold for years and years (paying management fees for years and years). I believe that market timing, however much luck plays a part, is at certain times in a stock market's life a significant factor in successful investing.

Being in—or out—of the market at certain times determines your success or failure. For three-quarters of the Dow's history, the market has recorded no progress and plenty of volatility. This past year, the Dow Jones Industrial Average celebrated its 100th birthday. The Dow, at its inception on May 26, 1896, had an opening price of 40.96. Thirty-six years later, on May 26, 1932, the Dow closed at 49.99. Through the 1930s, stock prices rose and fell (for example, from July 1932 to March 1937, the Dow climbed 380 per cent) but did not reach the levels of pre-Crash 1929 until 1954. In 1966, the Dow Jones index stood at 1000 points. Sixteen years later, in 1982, at the start of our current great bull market, the index was at 777.

Most people active in the markets in North America don't know this and, being in their forties and fifties, are really too young to have experienced anything but a major rising market. A bull market isn't just a phase, but, for the present crop of investors, a bull market is a generational assumption. Many investors have forgotten—or have never known—that the rules of the bull are the rules of a phase and exist only as long as the phase itself. They fail, or refuse, to recognize that markets run in cycles over a number of years, which cause prices to rise to a peak and then fall to a bottom before rising to another peak. When the markets make their sea change, the rules change as well. But within this current bull, it's worth remembering that investors who reduced their equity positions before the few short shakeouts that have occurred substantially outperformed those adhering to a buy-and-hold strategy, while at the same time reducing their exposure to risk.

The usual duration of a bear market is about one-third of the length of the preceding bull. With a bull market of fifteen years' duration and such gigantic gains already behind us, I expect that the lifespan of the coming bear market will put it into the next century. Beyond that, it will take many years to get equity prices back to the levels of today. Stockholders will be lucky to beat inflation over the next ten years.

Is there any good news? Yes. Learning the rules for a new invest-ment phase can mean financial survival and even further prosperity. For those who take their profits out of the market ahead of the peak and put their money out of harm's way, the buying opportunities in the future will be magnificent. By doing this, the smart investor will have accomplished the most important goal—preserving his or her wealth—and will be well placed to capitalize on the next inevitability: another bull market.

One of the biggest difficulties in a bear market is figuring out whether you are in a major free-fall or a minor correction. Selling in a major bear is smart; selling in the other is foolish. In October 1987, the market plunged 1000 points in a few weeks, and most of that drop was in its last three days. It was called a "crash" and was linked in many peo-ple's minds to the Crash of '29. But, for all its fury, it was in fact just a tremendous but brief correction. Within months, the market had bounced back, and since then the Dow has steamed steadily upwards. Thousands and thousands of investors, however, panicked in those first three terrifying weeks and sold their stocks and mutual funds at tremendous losses. The lesson they learned was not to panic, but to hold on and wait out any correction.

This is now the most dangerous piece of learning to be had in the stock market—especially for those investors whose retirement savings are at stake. When the bear makes his entrance, what will determine his ferocity is investors' willingness to buy the down ticks. I would guess that, in the first leg down, the buying will be aggressive. But how the markets behave in the subsequent rally will be the deciding factor. If the rally fails, watch out below.

This Time It's Not Different. Rather, it is time to wake up to the reality of this aging bull. I will show you why and how you can avoid making the biggest mistake of your investing career. The coming bear market will not be a "correction." When it comes, it will be a tidal wave, carrying everyone with it.

CHAPTER ONE

Raging Bull: How We Got Here

"Bull markets are born on pessimism, grow on skepticism, mature on optimism and die on euphoria."

—SIR JOHN TEMPLETON IN 1994

"It doesn't get much better than this!" That's what the chief market strategist for the esteemed New York investment house Smith Barney exclaimed to the Dow Jones News Service during a particularly buoyant week on the New York Stock Exchange in late February 1996.

At the time, the statement was greeted as confirmation that stocks had nowhere to go but up, that the flood of money coming into the stock market from mutual funds was a demographic certainty, that inflation had been licked for good, that an expanding global economy was ravenous for North America's goods and services, and all that, plus a faltering bond market, was happily conspiring to make the stock exchange a permanent nirvana for investors.

This made me nervous. Where was the so-called wall of worry that markets must climb if they are to continue to rise? It is commonly held in the dens and pens of Wall Street and Bay Street that as long as there are worries about the future of the market, of the economy, and of individual stocks, then a bull is sustainable because there is room for those worries to be unfounded and, consequently, for stock prices to move up. However, if the outlook is uniformly sunny for all, then stock prices should have nowhere to go but down. *It truly can't get any better than this.*

Throughout my career as an investor, trader, and arbitrageur, I have always made my money betting against what "everyone" thinks. As a confirmed contrarian, when I hear someone say something unequivocal, I tend to believe the opposite to be true. To me, that market strategist's ebullience was a cause for alarm. It was a classic statement of euphoria and, as such, likely heralded the coming market meltdown. Before the bear comes the euphoria, as history has demonstrated time and time again, whether it is the Dutch tulip-bulb mania of the 1630s or the American stock market of the 1920s or the craze for gold in the early 1970s. Unfortunately, however, as John Kenneth Galbraith has observed, there can be few fields of human endeavour in which history counts for so little as the world of finance.

Consider these two statements:

For the last five years we have been in a new industrial era in this country. We have been and still are in a period in which growth is not being made by the normal stages of development: we are making progress industrially and economically not even by leaps and bounds but on a perfectly heroic scale. (*Forbes*, June 1929)

I would like to propose a thesis that as the result of all that has been happening in the economy, the world and the market during the last decade, we are at least in a different—if not a new—era and the traditional thing, the standard approach to the market, is no longer in synchronization with the real world. (*Forbes*, October 1968)

Now consider what happened soon after those fearless predictions: Stock prices fell between September 1929 and June 1932 by 80 to 90 per cent. And stocks dropped nearly 60 per cent between December 1968 and December 1974. These were the two biggest secular bear markets of this century. So far.

Without a look back at the past, it would in fact be easy to conclude that, for stock market investors, it just doesn't get much better than it has been in the past few years. The market has set record after record. At one point in the banner year of 1995, the U.S. market hit eighteen straight weekly highs, and the Dow Jones Industrial Average smashed through the 4000 and 5000 barriers inside of ten months.

In mid-February of this year, the Dow cracked through the 7000 mark for the first time. The widely cited indicator, which measures the stock-price movements of thirty blue-chip companies trading in New York, wasn't the only one reaching a milestone. The Standard & Poor's (S&P) 500 stock index hit a record 811.82 points on the same day. And the Toronto Stock Exchange 300 composite index jumped above 6200 for the first time, to 6225.78, the second new high in a row. Around the world in early 1997, stock markets large and small hit new highs: London, Frankfurt, Mexico City, Sydney.

It was all part of a growing global equity culture. But the source of it was the steamrolling U.S. market. And whither it goes, others surely follow. Since the bull's beginnings in August 1982, the S&P 500 index (the best measure of the overall U.S. stock market) has gained 700 per cent. The Dow Jones Industrial Average—an index so ubiquitously used that it has become synonymous with "the market"—has skyrocketed 800 per cent.

Until recently (mid-March to mid-April 1997) the U.S. market had not suffered a setback of more than 10 per cent since late 1990. Even the June–July 1996 shakeup really produced only a 9.6 per cent decline on the Dow before the market resumed its upward path. Only twice before have we seen six years without a 10 per cent correction: in the 1920s and the 1960s. During both of those times, the economy was booming along and the general population was imbued with an enormous sense of optimism—not to mention a strong belief that the economy had entered a new era of unending expansion.

This current bull has defied logic and confounded sceptics. Back in early 1992, Forbes ran an article entitled "The Crazy Things People Say to Rationalize Stock Prices." It led with this statement: "We are in the midst of a speculative buying panic. Equities are $800 billion over-priced. Sometime between now and the end of the century, today's avid stock buyers will wake up very disappointed. All of their rationalizations and justifications of the early 1990s will look silly."

Well, the end of the century has yet to arrive, but the bull market in question has trampled over the jitters of 1992—and the four years that followed.

An entire generation active in the market today has never experienced a protracted period of declining stock prices. Whether individual investors, managers of pension or mutual funds, or strategists and brokers on Wall Street and Bay Street, they are the ones you have been reading about in the daily financial news who pronounce that "This Time It's Different" (TTID).

I believe: This Time It's Not Different. A severe bear market is inevitable, and on the horizon. Why? Well, the trigger could be anything, but it is usually something fundamental such as an across-the-board weakening of earnings or a hike in interest rates that is either unexpected or unexpectedly large or, as in the momentary market meltdown of October 1989, a major merger or takeover that suddenly fails. The determining factor on the bear's severity and duration, however, is found at the heart of the stock market: crowd psychology in action, the balance of fear and greed playing out against a background of financial assets. The TTID contingent can argue that baby-boomers, technological innovation, internationalization, and instant communications have produced structural changes in the market that ensure demand for stocks or ensure rising earnings or ensure further productivity gains. But in the end it is still the on-balance swings in the psychology of the crowd that dominates the action of the stock market.

Behind every single transaction, irrespective of individual motive or rationale, lie two basic human behavioural traits: fear and greed. As my friend Ian McAvity, the Toronto-based technical analyst who authors the newsletter *Deliberations*, likes to say: Nobody ever bought a stock hoping it would go down, and nobody ever sold a stock out of fear that it might go up.

This is the common thread that links the present and future markets with the past—despite all of the new innovative market instruments, and despite the refrain of "This Time It's Different." When markets start moving down, untested investors will react as they always have—despite the bravado exhibited recently in surveys published in *Barron's* and *Maclean's*. When the latter magazine asked mutual fund investors what they would do if there were a big crash, 56 per cent said they would maintain their holdings, 22 per cent said they would buy more, 8 per cent said they would reduce their holdings, and 3 per cent admitted they would sell all. That is bull-market talk. It is easy for them to say they will add more stock to their portfolios or hold firm. But, once the psychology changes, the individual will be drawn into the mass stampede for the exits.

All Gain, No Pain

On August 13, 1981, investors heard the siren call and began to fall under the spell of stocks and bonds. The Dow had dropped by 24 per cent in the sixteen months preceding, and over the previous decade investors had grown increasingly disillusioned with the stock market, despairing that the exhilarating high of 1000 points reached in 1968 would ever be surpassed. Even several sustained rallies during the 1970s failed to inspire in people the belief that a new investment cycle had begun. They stayed out of stocks.

But in September 1982, a bull market in long bonds commenced. The Federal Reserve in the United States, by dropping the discount rate, had heralded the end of the inflationary spiral that had plagued the economy and devastated the stock and bond markets throughout the 1970s.

It has been an extraordinary ride since then.

Secular bull markets have an overall upward trend. But within this trend are phases which are defined by corrections. In a bull market, the tops of each wave go higher and higher, with the lows of each wave progressively higher than previous lows. (The opposite is true of a bear market, where rallies top-out lower than previous rallies, and lows hit levels below previous lows.) When these speculative binges get going, they can gather incredible momentum and prove very profitable for some before they burn themselves out. This happened in 1968, when stock prices rose steeply and rapidly just ahead of the major bear of the 1970s.

There have been three main phases to this secular bull—from 1982 to 1987, from 1987 until 1990, and since October 1990: the biggest jet-fuelled surge. Overall, it has been fifteen years with nary a year where the low broke below the previous year's low. Stocks are trading at, near, or above all-time-high valuations relative to earnings, dividends, and book value. This phenomenon is worldwide. Extraordinary.

In the fall of 1987, we experienced in one week a free-fall in the markets (the S&P 500, for example, dropped 31.2 per cent). Although at the time it was a cataclysmic experience, with the "market meltdown" compared with the Great Crash of '29, it was, in reality, nothing more than a pullback on a powerful bull market. Within months, stock prices were back up to their pre-meltdown levels, and only those who sold off in paroxysms of fear—and there were plenty of them—lost money.

In 1990, during three months from mid-July to mid-October, markets tumbled 20 per cent (the Dow, 21 per cent; S&P, 20 per cent; TSE, 16 per cent) when Iraqi troops invaded Kuwait at the start of the Gulf War. Adding up the major reversals of this incredible bull in terms of months of decline, they are vastly below (less than half) the amount of time the two previous great bull markets of this century spent in corrections.

What's been driving the bull? The U.S. economy is in its seventh year of expansion and, more important, has managed to grow at just the right pace to sustain profitability without igniting inflationary fires. This is the so-called Goldilocks economy—not too hot, not too cold, just right. Just as important, interest rates declined steadily since 1982, and especially since the recession of 1989–90, as the central bankers who rule the world demonstrated that they had learned from their mistakes of the 1970s and that they were committed to price stability. By the same token, bond investors have become highly vigilant with respect to signs of inflation, and the bond market is quick to hike yields in order to exert some control over what it sees as irresponsible monetary and fiscal policies.

The absence of inflation forced business to become more competitive and productive. No longer could companies rely on it to mask the realities of its balance sheets. In the 1990s, relentless, merciless rounds of cost-cutting, downsizing, and job-axing along with a surge in the use of technology in all aspects of production combined to create enormous profitability and productivity—with the result that the economy went into a long-term expansion.

In the last few years, earnings growth has been lusty and has continued to justify a skyward-bound market, surprising many in the process. For example, when the Dow hit 4000 in late February 1995, the index's price-to-earnings (P/E) ratio was 15.6. Two years later, in February 1997, the Dow is up 75 per cent at 7000, but its P/E ratio is up less than 30 per cent. Corporate earnings in the United States have bumped up 29 per cent over the same period—and 50 per cent since 1994. In short, the market is outpacing earnings growth.

The persistent strong gains in the market and the short-lived nature of the few corrections that have occurred have emboldened individuals who were previously fearful of market risks to take a plunge into stocks. Unlike previous stock market booms going all the way back to the nineteenth century and as recent as the 1960s, when foreigners lapped up American stocks, this bull has been almost entirely a domestic affair. Lower levels of foreign investment in equities have easily been compensated for by stock-mad ordinary Americans.

1982–1987: The Run-Up

In 1982, the economy had just emerged from a severe recession, and a Third World debt crisis that had shaken North American banks. Long-term interest rates were extremely high as investors demanded a huge risk premium to protect themselves against a resurgence of the inflation that had plagued the economy during the 1970s. This early stage of the bull market was really a catch-up period as stocks rebounded from undervalued prices. It was the classic beginning of a secular bull market: abroad in the land was enormous pessimism about the long-range economic outlook, and widespread scepticism regarding equities as an investment. In fact, *Business Week* magazine became famous for publishing two cover stories: "The Death of Equities" and "The Death of Bonds," both of which appeared just as major bull markets in those securities began.

As a professional trader and investor, I made most of my money during the years 1982 to 1987. During that time, the market gained 300 per cent, with few headlines reporting on the market's rise and none talking about the public's financial mania. The reason is that, as is typical in the early stages of any major bull, it is mainly the professionals—the investment bankers, the acquisitors, and the arbitrageurs—who are reaping the profits, not the general public. During this stage, the bull market had to climb that proverbial wall of worry and fear. (Think, by contrast, of the U.S. market since 1994, where it has moved from record high to record high on one piece of good news after another.)

The second phase of the bull market began in the mid-1980s, when slumping oil prices and renewed fears of deflation resulted in a sharp drop in interest rates. What happened next was predictable enough: A surge in liquidity triggered a wave of financial speculation. Real estate prices soared; it was a heyday for takeover artists like the Belzberg brothers out of Vancouver, who made greenmail an artform for a while (scaring corporations with takeover threats and getting paid big bucks to go away); this was the era of Michael Miliken and junk bonds and escalating leveraged buyouts. The corporate appetite for riskier endeavours was matched by the public's appetite for riskier assets.

In early 1987 the Dow hit the 2000 mark, the TSE closed the same day at 3178, and the public stampeded into equities. In August the market peaked. The mania was feverish, and cabbies were experts on stocks. Some of the pros were nervous, and for the very reasons that some are nervous now.

The Crash of 1987

Leading up to the crash, the market had been getting frothier throughout the summer. On August 13, the TSE hit its high, at 4112.86. On August 25, the Dow Jones hit a record high of 2736, more than three times the level of August 12, 1982, the start of the bull. Markets in other countries were experiencing unprecedented rises as well. Tokyo and London marked levels three times higher than in August 1982. Price-to-earnings ratios were at historically high levels in New York, an average of twenty times higher, and above fifty for Japanese stocks.

Through September and early October, in New York, the market declined somewhat, occasionally knocking off record point drops, but always recovering. Trading volume was rising to record levels.

October 28, 1929, loomed large in the investor psyche, and there was fear in some quarters that price movements would repeat themselves. Just before the 1987 crash, the pattern of 1929 received a fair bit of attention, although economic variables and other things were rarely taken into account. Most notably, *The Wall Street Journal* actually ran an article on the very morning of the crash, on October 19, 1987, plotting stock prices in the 1920s and 1980s.

The crash arrived suddenly and largely unexpectedly. With a single downdraft over the course of a week, hundreds of billions of dollars were wiped out, and hordes of small investors were chased out of the market for the following several years—the very years when the market began a strong rise on relatively thin volume. (Remember that cynical Street chestnut: A bear market's purpose is to return money to its rightful owners. It reflects the view of many of those who work in the market that the individual or the unsophisticated investor is a "sucker," there for the taking by the "smart money.")

During two sessions, the Dow moved down more than 600 points, causing investors' blood to freeze in their veins and temporarily shaking the underpinnings of the American financial system. Later, Wall Street executives and regulatory bigwigs would pin the blame for the mess on unrestrained use of computerized program trading. But the real danger of such a collapse—that the credit foundations of the world's largest economic power were at risk—was never properly confronted by those in authority.

On October 14, the U.S. trade deficit number was announced, and at $30 billion it was precisely double what had been expected. Japanese holders of U.S. Treasury bonds began to sell. The Dow Jones gave up 95 points that day. Two days later, sophisticated index and equity options trading strategies employed by major institutional traders expired and the Dow lost more than 100 points in one day. It wiped out $145 billion worth of equity capital from the value of the largest U.S. companies.

Over the weekend, market players bit their fingernails and downed Maalox as they contemplated the coming week. On Sunday, October 18, and into early Monday, the Tokyo market started to drop, ending down 2.35 per cent. Other overseas exchanges were even worse off. On "Bloody Monday," October 19, the New York market was slammed down 300 points in the morning, and 508 by close of trading—down 22 per cent from Friday's close, and 36 per cent from the August high. Huge corporate names saw their share prices simply melt away: Disney went from $65^{1}/$_{8}$ to $46^{1}/$_{8}$ and Eastman Kodak dropped from $89^{1}/$_{2}$ to $63^{1}/$_{2}$—all in the course of one day. New York Stock Exchange market specialists were hit with thousands of sell offers and no one wanting to buy at any price. An astounding 604 million shares changed hands that day, three times the NYSE daily average volume for the year. Fund managers, who thought they could rely on so-called portfolio insurance (strategies that called for the disciplined selling of stock futures to compensate for declines in the underlying equity market), found out otherwise and panicked. In the face of such enormous market drops, they sold stocks rather than futures contracts, and also sold futures at huge discounts to cash.

The decline was not limited to blue-chips, either. The over-the-counter market, NASDAQ, fell more than 11 per cent, prices on the American Stock Exchange (AMEX) dropped 12 per cent, both on record volume. In Toronto, the index fell 407 points, or 11.3 per cent.

Tuesday morning, the New York market took wild swings on near-record volume, shooting up 200 points, then down 227 points, then back up 120 points, to close up 102 points, a 5.8 per cent increase. However, overseas markets continued to be pummelled, Toronto fell almost 7 per cent and the U.S. market indexes for smaller stocks declined further. Even a full week after the start of the meltdown, the astounding volume of trading and the volatility endured in almost every market.

The post-crash analysis of why the market meltdown had occurred was generally unsatisfying. Immediately following the turmoil, the Reagan Administration set up the Brady Commission to investigate the causes of the crash and to map out exactly what had happened and when. Popular targets of blame were institutionalized trading, which had come to dominate the market, and computerized trading, those newfangled financial instruments that caused tremendous gyrations and "triple witching hours." Much was also made of the links between the "real" stock market in New York and the futures market in Chicago and the minuscule price and timing differences that are exploited by traders for millions of dollars.

"Those who favored efficient market explanations—fundamental economic reasons for every kind of market move—had a difficult time with the historic downturn," wrote Mark Fadiman in *Rebuilding Wall Street*. The Brady Commission, however, seemed to imply the opposite: "The crash had been the product of a classic, speculative-type bubble that had ballooned in the 1980s and, aggravated by program trading, had finally burst."

It is my belief that, despite the devastation caused by the programmed and panicked selling, that crash will be seen as generous to investors when we experience a true bear-market break. By the end of October, the market had regained its staggering losses and once again smashed through 2000 on the Dow. The lesson from the Crash of '87 was: ride out the downdrafts.

Because the market recovered so quickly, the effect on investors was to reinforce the conviction that the only investment strategy that pays off is that of buying in the pullbacks and remaining as fully invested as possible. That strategy is terrific when you are talking about quick-and-dirty market drops. But that strategy can really hurt in a prolonged downturn.

Recession and Recovery

A brutal recession took hold of North America in 1989. Real estate (including family homes) plummeted in value, wiping out unrealized equity. Plants closed. Jobs disappeared. Retailers and the malls that housed them shuttered their doors. The flashy, trashy, wealthy, BMW-driving '80s had come to a close.

Aside from the 20 per cent shocker caused by Iraq invading Kuwait, the scene was set for the market mania of the 1990s as the U.S. Federal Reserve massively eased monetary policy. This was one of the most stimulative monetary expansions of the post–Second World War peri-od as the central bank responded to the collapse in real estate values and a threatened banking sector. As short-term rates fell, investors once again moved their money into stocks and bonds, disregarding the increased risk as they pursued higher returns, and growth in mutual funds exploded. More than 80 per cent of all current investors in mutu-al funds got into them after 1990. And as their risk tolerance grew, investors also began speculating in the more exotic: emerging markets, mortgage-backed securities, and derivatives. (The last mentioned, which received some bad press for amplifying gyrations in the market, are financial instruments that derive their value from some underlying asset such as a commodity, a debt security, a currency, an equity, or an index, and are sold in the form of options or futures or swaps. Derivatives are both publicly and privately traded, often changing hands second by second, or minute by minute, and some transactions are so complex their value can only be estimated using copyrighted computer models.)

Investors began bidding up equity prices in the hopes of a resurgent economy. (Their wish was finally granted in 1996 and it may well mean the end of their enchantment with stocks.) Bond markets everywhere soared to levels not seen since President Richard Nixon closed the gold window in 1971. With the genie of inflation back in the bottle, the bond market found a genie beyond Aladdin's dreams: economic growth without credit growth. For owners of stocks and bonds, it was the best of times. For the unemployed, it was the worst of times. Even for those with jobs (unless they were in the financial sector), it was a time of con-tinuing insecurity amid corporate and public downsizing.

As liquidity floated the world's capital markets, 1993 was a good year. The Dow finished up almost 14 per cent, Toronto up an amazing 29 per cent. But it was a year for investors, not workers, as the recession dragged on in Canada and vicious downsizing spread across North America.

The following year, the American market saw rough sailing as finan-cial scandals beset the exotic markets—among them, the Orange County derivatives scandal (in which the county pension fund lost billions on derivative speculation) and the dive in the Mexican stock market. Still, investors continued to pour money into funds, and their confidence in stocks remained strong as they bought on weakness. In Toronto, the market, plagued by international worries over the Quebec referendum and lagging economic growth, was erratic but ended down 2.5 per cent.

Amid that commotion, however, corporations in North America were finally beginning to see the fruits of their years-long effort to downsize, invest in technology, and compete globally. Earnings were about to take off. The stage was set for the mania to come.

By June it was clear that 1995 was an auspicious year for the New York markets. So much so, in fact, that on June 19 *Forbes* headlined a story "How to Love the Market and Stop Worrying," the gist of which was that investors should continue to pour their money into stocks because, even if the market dropped in value by one-third—as it had in past bear markets—it was still the best place to invest. In a similar vein, the same week *The Wall Street Journal* argued that the bull had a long run left because "there is no structural imbalance in the economy." *Business Week* chimed in at the same time and ebulliently declared, in "The Amazing Ride Isn't Over Yet," that any correction, should one occur, would be short-lived.

They were right. The Dow surged ahead 33.5 per cent in 1995, thereby adding more than $1 trillion to the market value of the thirty stocks on that index. It set sixty-nine record-high closes. The S&P soared 34 per cent and set seventy-six new highs. The year ranked twelfth among the great bullish years of history for the S&P, going back to the American Civil War. It was the best year since 1958, and the third best since the Second World War. In Toronto, the 300 composite index managed a 12 per cent gain and sixty-four new highs, one-third more than in any other year.

Overall, 1995 not only delighted market watchers, but also surprised them. They hadn't counted on the amount of money investors shovelled into mutual funds in both nations as rates fell with the changing outlook for inflation. The U.S. inflation rate dropped below 3 per cent, the average going back to the turn of the century, and it emboldened them.

Most experts had been uniformly bearish at the start of the year, weighing in with dour predictions of a lacklustre market. But, as is often the case with the stock market, when popular consensus calls for one thing, the opposite holds true. In other words, the market soared in part simply because nobody expected it to; but, just as important, the massive liquidity injected by the Japanese banks into the U.S. market sent stock prices powering higher. Analysts and strategists found instead that they had a new thing to worry about and pontificate over: the unrestrained optimism and penchant for speculation that were amply evident.

A bubble in Internet-related stocks blew across equity markets and it was an extraordinary thing to behold. Prices for stocks in companies producing—or purporting to produce—software to help consumers navigate the vast Internet rocketed into cyberspace in late 1995. It was not uncommon for these stocks to double in three months. Many of them traded at more than fifteen times annualized revenues. Not a few that went public tripled their initial public offering (IPO) price. One was Premisys Communications, up 473 per cent from its IPO price by the end of 1995. Probably the most famous (indeed, it became synonymous with Net Madness) was Netscape Communications, which opened its first day of trading with a notional market value of more than $2 billion. The IPO had been originally priced at between $12 and $14, went to market at $28, and shot up to $74.76 on the first day. Eventually the stock traded 368 per cent above its IPO price—all this for a little company selling "browser" software for the Internet. The high-tech stocks, particularly those of companies with even the remotest connection to the Information Highway, promised the new pot of gold for investors.

Indeed, at the high-technology sector's high point in late 1995, the market capitalization of the small Internet-related companies reached $34 billion, exceeding the combined capitalization of MCI Communications and Sprint.

The numbers represented nothing more than rampant, frenzied speculation by "investors," mainly the big mutual funds seeking ever-higher performance numbers. The presence of Fidelity's giant Magellan Fund, for example, was the biggest factor in the high-tech sector when those stocks went through the roof during 1995.

As with most manias, there was a legitimate reason for optimism in the high-tech sector—the potential applications for the Internet and the new information age were limitless—but as time went on, the valuations grew wilder, and the rationalizations used to justify them more absurd. When the bubble bursts, as it did with technology stocks in mid-1996, it does so with a bang. There was precedent for this mania in the biotech and health stocks of the early 1990s, when irrational multiples were made rational with much talk about positive fundamentals, and billions flowed into biotech and health-care equity funds from infatuated investors. That bubble burst, too, and investors moved on to their next favourite sector. It reflected the rapacious attitude of the market, where the professional investors, especially the funds, move like a pack of coyotes to feed on one quarry and then, when it has been picked over for profit, move on to the next.

All of the action on Wall Street had little to do with Main Street. The huge and easy financial gains to be made in the stock market were not to be found in the real economy, where things are produced and sold and consumed. Wages certainly were not keeping up with stock gains. According to one calculation, a manufacturing worker had to labour for 49.2 hours to earn enough money to buy a unit of the S&P 500—the highest since the 1920s. In 1980, near the start of the bull, it took fifteen hours of toil. What was at work here was not just a meteoric rise in the market, but also a steady decline in workers' wages over the same period of time. Wall Street was on a bull run, but Main Street was lagging. Bay Street failed to match its New York counterpart, but the Canadian economy was even more anemic, with retail sales, housing starts, capital investment, job creation, and consumer confidence all mired in hopeless gloom. The problems of the recent past—Quebec, the deficit, unending layoffs, and relatively high interest rates—continued to overhang the economy.

The Top

Last year, 1996, had the three essentials: wonderful earnings, low interest rates, and high cash flow. The Canadian stock market finally broke out in 1996, and Toronto rose 26 per cent. The New York market gained 33 per cent.

With the higher returns came hordes of new investors. Many of them were what one executive at the Toronto-based investment firm Midland Walwyn Inc. dubbed "GIC refugees." These were investors who normally would be happy to put their money into GICs or other safe, interest-bearing instruments. But in 1996, GICs were offering 2.5 per cent for one year, a paltry amount roughly equal to inflation. These latecomers, however, weren't necessarily enthusiastic, or even knowledgeable, about the stock market. They simply felt they had nowhere else to put their money. "The market has been plumbing the depths of unsophistication to find new investors," observed Robert Prechter, Jr., who has been predicting an extremely deep and pro-tracted bear market for a couple of years now. (The fact that he's been premature in his prediction has undermined his credibility in some circles. But I believe he is one of the great market technicians—which doesn't make him infallible or right all the time, but does mean that his views should be part of a wide and varied input to anyone's invest-ment decision making.)

In the United States, small-cap stocks were all the rage, with indexes weighted towards small-caps setting one record after another. The NASDAQ composite index gained 13 per cent in the first four months, helped also by trading in large-caps such as Microsoft and Intel.

That is, until early summer, when the mutual funds, and in partic-ular Fidelity's huge Magellan Fund, moved out of the technology sec-tor, instantly draining it of its momentum. Over a three-week period in July, the Dow fell 9.6 per cent, and investors moved en masse into large-cap stocks like Coca-Cola, which they deemed "safer."

The pace of stock trading last year was frenetic on all the Canadian exchanges—in Toronto it jumped 43 per cent, to $351.3 billion, reflecting a year of successive index highs. What fuelled the Canadian market last year depended on when and where. In the West and in the first half of the year, investors were in the grip of penny-mining-stock fever brought on by the fabulous wealth creat-ed by Diamond Fields' Voisey's Bay nickel find and Bre-X's pur-ported Indonesian gold discovery. But, in the latter half of the year, the TSE took off when the big bank stocks began behaving more like penny stocks, with their stock prices skyrocketing by about 50 per cent. The big banks make up 15 per cent of the TSE 300 index, so how they perform often dictates the performance of the broader market. The TSE also began to enjoy the attentions of U.S. investors prowling for values.

Early in the year, Americans were astounding market watchers by throwing an average of $25 billion a month into mutual funds, twice the rate previously claimed as a record. In June and July, when the market sold off sharply, that flow suddenly dried up. But what looked at first like a full-scale retreat from stocks turned out to be strictly a summer vacation, and they were soon back buying funds enthusiastically. Canadian fund buyers behaved much the same way, piling as much as $7 billion into funds in a single month.

By August, fund sales and the market itself were back in high gear, and in mid-October the Dow closed above 6000 points for the first time. Through November, the Dow surged ahead without a pause for breath, setting records daily in the rally following the re-election of U.S. president Bill Clinton and a Republican Congress. In one week alone, the Dow recorded a whopping gain of 5.4 per cent.

"People who were reluctant to buy stock [when the Dow was] at 3500 are now buying them at the speed of light at 6300," marvelled Charles Clough, chief market strategist at Merrill Lynch & Co. to *The Wall Street Journal.* "It's a momentum market, a market driven by cash inflows, but I'm not sure that it's an investor's market at these levels."

It was no surprise, then, that in early December, Alan Greenspan, the chairman of the U.S. Federal Reserve Board, while delivering a dinner speech, chose to send a message to Wall Street. In a few carefully phrased sentences, he warned of the dangers of "irrational exuberance" in the market and lent the impression he might act to curb it. That was all it took. In what became known as the "Greenspan effect," the following day the Dow was knocked down 145 points in early trading, and a wave of selling rippled through stock markets in Asia and Europe and, of course, Canada. The bull spirit triumphed, however, and investors large and small, all of them trained on six years of untarnished markets to view declines as buying opportunities, snapped up stocks at their lows. At the day's end, the Dow was down "only" 55 points on the day, and within two months had stormed through the 7000-point level. Toronto closed down 32 points.

In late February 1997, the Fed chairman again attempted to curb the euphoria—the irrepressible Dow had risen 8.5 per cent since his December remarks—when he spoke before the U.S. Senate banking committee: "History demonstrates that participants in financial markets are susceptible to waves of optimism. Excessive optimism sows the seeds of its own reversal in the form of imbalances that tend to grow over time." His intention was to raise the idea of returning inflation and a hike in interest rates, although he never explicitly went near that. Many investors and traders found it hard to believe he would raise rates simply to prick a stock bubble. Still, his midmorning remarks triggered an instant 100-point drop in the Dow. The plunge reached nearly 123 points, but then a rally took hold and the close was down 55 points. Toronto ended the day down 46.35 points, and Greenspan's words also pushed down markets in Britain, France, Italy, and Sweden. Bond markets also fell.

The most interesting aspect of Greenspan's remarks, however, was his evocation of history as a caution to investors. He referred to the widespread belief that the stock market had entered a new era of low risk. "Regrettably, history is strewn with visions of such 'new eras' that in the end have proven to be a mirage. In short, history counsels caution. Such caution seems especially warranted with regard to the sharp rise in equity prices during the past two years. These gains have raised questions of sustainability." Then he raised the subject of mania: "It's not the markets that are irrational; it's the people who become irrationally exuberant on occasion and take actions that induce what economists like to call bubbles, which eventually burst."

Euphoria

Robert Sobel, a professor of business history at Hofstra University, has written at length on the bull markets of the 1920s and 1960s. He knows what he is talking about. He calls the current bull market "the most stock-stricken period in American history." And although much has changed since the great bull market of the 1920s, he notes, "in raw volume, the equity business of the 1920s was a flicker compared with the current market bonfire. There are more investors—large and small—trading a wider variety of issues these days than ever before."

It is a stock-mad world. In the past few years, the New York Stock Exchange average daily volume has more than tripled, to more than 400 million shares, and the number of companies listed has almost doubled, to 2,800. In Canada, the value of trading on the TSE topped $300 billion for 1996, improving on the previous year by nearly $100 billion. As well, every business day in 1996, an average $1.2 billion worth of shares changed hands on the exchange, more than double the volume only three years earlier. There was a record number of people working in the investment industry in Canada. And, in the United States, the number of brokerage houses had doubled from 1990.

The mania for equities has spread to extremely dangerous places. After a report that the American social security system would be bankrupt by 2029, the U.S. government looks like it will loosen investment restrictions for the social security trust fund and open them up to the stock market instead of only to government securities. The Canadian government went one better when it revamped the Canada Pension Plan in early 1997; a key but small section of the reform package allowed future contributions to the plan's reserve fund to be put into stocks instead of only provincial bonds. This is true madness, coming at the top of a bull market—especially a bull already fed by the fears of those facing retirement.

Investors are behaving even more irrationally than usual. The adage of buying stocks when they are cheap and selling when they are dear no longer applies. Today's investor—the man or woman in the market since 1990—has been buying expensive stocks, hoping to sell them at an even higher price to someone else. It's the "greater fool" theory. Or worse, this new investor has no intention of selling at all, being a long-term investor; however, most people's idea of the long term is not some place well past their age of retirement.

The investment landscape abounds with unhealthy symptoms, speculative fever, rampant bullishness, a scorn for risk, and mass silliness—all of it very typical of the blow-off stage of a bull market.

The best illustration of this euphoria is the proliferation of initial public offerings, most of them lapped up by investors at insane valuations. "Air balls," the columnist Alan Abelson calls them.

Planet Hollywood was one, a chain of restaurants with movie stars Melanie Griffith, Demi Moore, Arnold Schwarzenegger, and Sylvester Stallone as stockholders and as the main attraction. The Planet went public in April 1996 at $18, and immediately soared to $32 before settling back at $26. Its market capitalization at the time was $2.7 billion—nine times sales and a hundred times earnings! With twenty-four company-owned outlets and six franchises, that meant that the market had placed a value of $91 million for each restaurant.

Embassy Acquisitions was another: Its prospectus admitted it had no plans for the $8.28(US) million it raised, but it got the public to pay $6 a share where insiders had paid $0.06. In high-tech stocks, buyers last year were paying absurd multiples—up to a century of earnings for a stock—for upstart outfits like Iomega (P/E ratio of 348) and Presstek (P/E of 736).

There were other signs of an insane and topping-out market: an Internet market for shares in dubious companies, themed mutual funds. All of these things start to appear when investor attention shifts away from fundamentals to dreams of the future.

The mania in evidence in the United States for technology issues was matched in Canada with the mining and exploration sector. In both cases, unrealized potential was the quarry of investors, and the hunt for it drove tiny companies run by unknowns to absurd market capitalizations, taking the market with them. This, of course, also opened the door to shaky ventures, and even downright scams, as greed and the need to earn higher and higher rates of return blinded even the most sophisticated market players.

As the junior resource stocks rocketed up, Canadian mutual funds, who got in early, became red-hot performers for their clients—one feeding the other. The action later attracted heavy interest from American investors—which further fed the bidding frenzy. Some of the excitement was legitimate, such as that over Diamond Fields

Resources Inc.'s mammoth nickel find at Voisey's Bay in Labrador. Diamond Fields traded at $3.37 at the end of 1994, hit $25.75 at year-end 1995 (for a gain of 663 per cent), and closed 1996 at $42.80. Until recently, Bre-X Minerals Ltd. was another story-book stock. On the strenght of the company's claim to have found a fabulous gold deposit in Indonesia, Bre-X went from $0.28 at the end of 1994 to $53 precisely one year later (a gain of 1,793 per cent!) to $21.70 at year-end 1996, adjusting for splits.

Those stock plays caused individual investors and institutions to scramble to get on "the next Bre-X." Which is how Cartaway Resources Corp. came to public attention. At its height, the market value was more than $700 million, pulling the Vancouver Stock Exchange up 100 per cent on the year. But Cartaway, which also traded on the Alberta Stock Exchange (ASE), had yet to release assays from its most promising property. The frenzy was based strictly on visual estimations of core samples. A mining analyst in Vancouver put it well when he said at the time, "For somebody to go and buy Cartaway stock in the $23 range based on visual estimates was ludicrous." True as that was, there was simply too much money pumping into the system and too much greed driving it, much of it from the unsophisticated investor—the kind, worried the analyst, who might take out a second mortgage to buy Cartaway.

The Cartaway saga was a classic bubble—as well as a foreshadow of things to come for Bre-X. The chair of the Alberta Securities Commission, William Hess, said it succinctly: "You've got an overheated market with wild, wild swings to every word that is being said. Our job is to make sure that appropriate things are being said, but the reaction or overreaction to them, there's nothing we can do about that. We would love investors to take a sober second look at everything and not jump too quickly, but that's not the nature of the marketplace right now."

The inevitable of course happened. On May 21, 1996, Cartaway's shares plunged from $23 to $2.78 in the first few minutes of trading. The stock instantly became one of the biggest flameouts in Canadian exchange history. Six million shares changed hands on the ASE, which was completely incapable of coping with the meltdown. (The same thing happened to the much larger Toronto Stock Exchange almost a year later, when Bre-X collapsed.) In fact, the first of the bad news about Cartaway's drilling results came out on the Friday before a long weekend, but trading was halted because the exchange couldn't keep up with the volume. Those trades that did make it through—taking the stock price from $23 to $6.50—were nullified and, after emergency weekend computer repairs, the exchange reopened on Tuesday after the holiday.

The fallout hit other stocks whose principal allure for investors had been their proximity to Diamond Fields' property at Voisey's Bay. Canadian State Resources Inc., in which I held some shares, dropped from $5.50 the previous week to $2. (I had purchased my shares at $0.45 and sold half my stake at between $3 and $4. The share price at one point reached $7, but I stayed in; after the stock collapsed, I sold out at $2—still making a tidy return.) By this time, the mutual funds had taken their massive profits, and although some lost significantly, it hardly made a dent in their annual returns.

The most profitable, most damaging, and most fantastic stock saga of all turned out to be that of Bre-X, whose share price dropped from the $20 range to as low as $1.76 in the early months of 1997. As I write this, it is still not clear exactly what the truth is about the gold find at Busang in Indonesia, but it has provided investors with a sharp reminder that value can disappear in minutes on the stock exchange.

The speculative frenzies erupting in the North American stock markets through 1995 and 1996 were redolent of another mania in the "soaring '60s," the bull market that preceded the bear that began in 1969, and subsequently took a bad turn in 1973. In the early part of the decade, the "tronics" boom captured investors' imaginations. Companies such as Vulcatron and Circuitronics and Space-Tone suddenly appeared on the scene—often the jazzed-up new names of otherwise mundane enterprises. The "tronics" boom, as Burton Malkiel notes in his book *A Random Walk on Wall Street*, came to a sudden end in 1962 during a market break that saw the growth stocks evaporate while the rest of the market just plunged. Later in the decade, during another bout of mania, "concept" stocks such as Polaroid and Xerox took the market by storm just as the competition among institutional investors intensified. The funds were desperate for anything

that would put their numbers higher than their rivals'. (Sound familiar?) As a result, the funds bought into anything labelled a concept—including the famous Minnie Pearl's chicken franchises, which had been renamed Performance Systems. The stock's price-to-earnings multiple was a mystery because the company had no earnings at all to divide into the price at the time it reached its high in 1968. As if he were speaking today, Malkiel wrote: "When the 1969–71 bear market came, these concept stocks went down just as fast as they went up. In the end it was the pros who were conned most of all. While there is nothing wrong with seeking good performance, the mad rush to outgun the competition week by week had disastrous consequences."

Malkiel goes on to describe the mêlée: "By 1959 the traditional rule that stocks should sell at a multiple of 10 to 15 times their earnings had been supplanted by multiples of 50 to 100 times earnings, or even more for the glamorous issues. For example, in 1961 Control Data sold for over 200 times its previous year's earnings … These prices could not be justified on firm-foundation principles. But investors firmly believed that later in the wonderful decade of the 60s, buyers would eagerly come forward to pay even higher prices."

The lessons of the past are largely lost on the market participants of the present. Most people working on Wall Street and Bay Street aren't old enough to have learned those lessons first-hand and are not inclined to make a study of them. Instead, they form their conclusions about the market based on three things: earnings forecasts, the economic outlook, and market sentiment of the moment. However, some veteran market watchers like *Barron's* Alan Abelson have grown increasingly nervous as the incline on the Dow has steepened. (Against such a backdrop of bullishness and boosterism, they come across as curmudgeons.)

The anecdotal evidence—"sentiment," as it's known in the market—was just as discomfiting. For me, the Sotheby's auction of Jackie Onassis's possessions in April 1996 in New York neatly paralleled the action across town on Wall Street. A bidding frenzy developed for very ordinary household possessions dating from the "Camelot" Kennedy era. A tape measure went for $48,875, a humidor given to Jack Kennedy by Milton Berle went for $574,400. The esteemed auction house had vastly underestimated what those two items—and everything else—would go for. Their original valuations had been $500–$700 and $2,000–$2,500, respectively.

The incredible gap between true value and market value illustrated by the Sotheby's event—which even made the top of the news most places—raised the philosophical question of why people pay outlandish prices for things of much lesser worth. Buyers at the Jackie O. auction were animated by what Alan Abelson has called "refracted celebrity"; buyers in the stock market, by greed. Both marketplaces speak to the psychology of investing, and how different the thing sought is from the thing bought. Part of what makes the thing sought so "valuable" is the degree to which a frenzy for it develops, and that is as effectively achieved by word of mouth as by pronouncements by experts. But for the thing sought to soar in price far beyond its true value, you need not only a market gone mad with desire, but also a temper of the times so strong that it is no longer confined to a rarefied group. You need to have even the "ordinary Joe" picking up on the mania and acting.

Such was the case in the stock market of 1996, when traditional, conservative investment mindsets had been all but completely dispensed with. One equities trader was quoted as saying: "Six months ago, a 100-point drop would have scared accounts out of the market for a month. Now they want to play the moves. Volatility is the rule." That was on a day when the Dow ended down 71 points. A crash normally sends people selling; fund managers, arbitrageurs, and individuals usually want to get out at any price. But in New York and Toronto, volumes were quite light, such was the confidence level of investors. This demonstrates, to me at least, that there were too many money managers believing they will have time to exit a seriously crashing market and that the investing public didn't have exiting on their radar screen.

Yet the "smart money" was selling. Insider selling had been increasing significantly, and while the high-tech stocks were booming in late 1995, insiders were selling heavily. And what were we to make of Warren Buffett, the greatest living investor in America, when, in May 1996, his legendary company, Berkshire Hathaway, issued class-B shares at $1,100 a piece. (The so-called Baby Berkshires were a supposed bargain compared with the regular shares, which were going for $33,500 each.) Demand for Buffett's company was so great that the pricey shares sold out immediately. No one stopped to ask: Why is this supremely savvy investor selling when the rest of us are buying?

This is not to say there wasn't nervousness. The gluttony was mixed with some trepidation. Traders on some days were afraid to take bathroom breaks in case the market started to crack. Wild rumours moved the market. One Friday in the fall of 1996, a rumour swept through Wall Street that Abby Joseph Cohen, the stock market strategist at Goldman Sachs & Co. and a stalwart bull, had backed away from her long-held view that the Dow was poised to go significantly higher. That rumour— which turned out to be utterly false—contributed to a huge retreat in the Dow that day. Cohen even had to put a voice-mail recording on her phone, saying: "For those of you who are calling to check whether we have changed our view on the U.S. stock market, the answer is no."

I believe we are completing a major top, which will probably play out to 7500 to 8000 points on the Dow and 6500 to 7000 on the TSE. This will mark the end of a great bull market. It's as difficult to detect when you are at the top of a market as it is to determine when you are at the bottom. Judging either correctly is the key to making money or losing it. And, of course, after you've passed the top or the bottom, it is very easy to identify in hindsight.

By many traditional measures of value, the stock market has been overvalued for some time. Even with the correction of March 1997, I believe pressure is growing for a conventional bear market.

Ask yourself what makes the actual top or bottom in the market. Every transaction that occurs has a buyer on one side and a seller on the other. Every price change—up or down—is implicitly driven by one or the other "reaching" to make the trade occur. In other words, the buyer reaches up to motivate a transaction or the seller reaches down to hit a bid. In this sense, the actual high and low points can be characterized as those at which the last buyer bought or the last seller sold.

This, of course, is an oversimplification. But if you see the market as the central forum for millions of buyers and millions of sellers, that is how the actual extreme occurs. Nobody knows exactly when that moment happens until after the fact.

This third great bull market of the twentieth century has taken stock indexes to new, stratospheric highs. Bulls say there is a reason for all of this: sound reason, rather than speculative mania. Of course, as scholars and historians such as John Kenneth Galbraith have pointed out many times, speculation is at its most dangerous when those doing the speculating don't realize that they are speculating, not investing. No one readily admits to manic behaviour.

As this is written, I do not see a whole lot of energy left to play the markets much longer. The bottom-fishing is poor. People are saying, "I would love for the market to go down 10 or 20 per cent so I could really get in." But obviously something changes in the dynamics between the top and the bottom for that not to happen.

Far more than earnings growth, the plunge in interest rates is what has carried this bull along for so long. Sooner or later, however, low interest rates will not be enough to conceal from investors the historically insane valuations in this market. (At that point, as with other times in history, stock prices will have dropped, regardless of the level of interest rates.)

The market is running out of steam. The regular surpassing of "all-time highs" by the Dow and other indexes has been exciting, but appearances are deceiving. It took the Dow forty years to hit the 1000 mark (on November, 14, 1972). By early January 1987 it had broken 2000—and broke through it again at the end of that year following the October crash. Hitting the milestones, however, has become easier with each passing one, simply because of the mathematics.

When the Dow advanced from 5000 to 6000, it achieved a 20 per cent gain. When it moved from there to 7000, the gain was 16.7 per cent. Clearly, the greatest gains are behind us.

I mentioned at the start of this chapter the euphoria expressed by the chief market strategist for Smith Barney early in 1996. A year later, when the Dow cracked 7000, it was another heady time for the bulls. And another New York market strategist—this one from Prudential Securities Inc.—crowed: "How high can it go? Dream your impossible dream—anything is possible."

CHAPTER TWO

Why the Bull Is Doomed: This Time It's Not Different

"The crowd has never thirsted for the truth. It turns aside from evidence that is not to its taste, preferring to glorify and to follow error, if the way of error appears attractive enough, and seduces them."
—GUSTAVE LEBON, A NINETEENTH-CENTURY OBSERVER OF CROWD PSYCHOLOGY

Harry D. Schultz is a market-newsletter pundit I like to read for his sage, contrarian, and irascible views. More than thirty years ago, he wrote one of the few books ever produced on bear markets, and he opened his 1964 missive with this story: A steel magnate looked out his office window at the rows of smoking factory chimneys, contemplated the healthy pile of unfilled orders on his desk, sent a memorandum to his production assistant to hire a hundred more men, and called his stockbroker to sell all the stocks he owned. "Are you crazy?" asked the broker. "No," said the magnate. "In all my years the future for our business has never looked as good as it does right now. Therefore I must assume that from now on it can only look worse."

Now consider the words of that Wall Street denizen who exclaimed, "It doesn't get much better than this!" Clearly he, and most others in the market today, haven't read Schultz or any other writer with a long-term outlook. They generally rely instead on their earnings forecasts for the next quarter, or two or three; their firm's economic outlook; and their reading of the market sentiment of the moment.

Of course, to be fair, most people today are sadly deluded about the stock market. They base their views on their personal experience— always a dangerous thing. The stock market, for most people, has been a very pleasant place to be for the past fifteen years. There have been only two violent shakeouts of the kind that prevail in a bear market (1987 and 1990). And they were sharp and short, with fast market recoveries. Overriding them is the simple fact that, if you stayed with good-quality stocks or index averages during this bull, you've made ten times your money. Standard & Poor's units (on the futures market), if bought in 1987 at the bottom, went for $216 apiece. At time of writing they're each worth $820. That's a return of more than 400 per cent in nine years by doing nothing but holding indexes. (As an aside, when the market crashed on October 19, 1987, I remember watching the tape all day, while losing a lot of money. But, at one point, the S&P futures hit $196 and there was a huge block held by the legendary George Soros waiting to be sold. Everyone in the market knew, and they held on, waiting for him to make his move. He finally sold it—at $181, which, as a futures contract, was a huge discount to the market. That block acted like magic: once it was out of the way, the market started moving up, and it marked the very bottom. At the time of the crash, Soros was long in the United States and short in Japan, and he was very wrong on both calls, which shows that even the sagest, smartest money manager in the world can make big misjudgements.)

Given the performance of the market in the 1990s, it's no wonder that most people who manage money have come to believe they are geniuses, and that the millions of dollars they are earning is the proof of that. Galbraith once termed it "the specious association of money and intelligence."

The dislocation that can happen in the market is not known to these players. Somehow they have two convictions. One, the market can only go up. Two, if the market happens to go down, it will be a short setback and, more important, a buying opportunity. In other words, the message is: "You can't get hurt." They have sold themselves and they have sold their clients on the notion that the market is a rational thing.

This has been drilled into people by financial institutions selling mutual funds and by many popular books promoting stocks as the only viable long-term way to make money.

Most people today are willing to believe these things precisely because they are in the market today rather than yesterday; they were not around for the great bear markets of the twentieth century. Their experience is limited to one of the greatest bull markets of this century.

A bull market like this happens once in a generation, but so does a vicious bear. In this century, there have been three great bulls—1924–29, 1949–68, and 1982 to the present—and three great bears—1929–32 (the one that started with a great crash), 1946–49 (the sideways bear), and 1969–74 (the one that ended with a crash).

Over the course of this century there have also been a great many declines of varying severity. A study by Ned Davis Research of Nokomis, Florida, on all declines in the Dow of 5 per cent or more since 1900 shows 318 such declines—an average of 3 a year. Absolutely routine. In the same period, drops of 30 per cent from the prior year's high have occurred every 4.6 years on average. And worse, declines of 40 per cent came every 8.7 years.

The rallying cry for bulls and sales people in the mutual fund industry is: Stocks always go up. The word "eventually" should be added to that statement. Here are some examples, calculated by Ian McAvity, of stocks taking an awfully long time to go up:

- The investor who bought the S&P in 1906 (actually it was a predecessor index) at 10 points saw that level again in 1941. Between those two dates, the S&P was up as high as 31.92 in 1929 and as low as 4.04 in 1932. You could have counted on terrific market timing. Or, you could have been in for the long term—and had to wait thirty-five years to be even.
- If an investor bought within 10 per cent of the top in 1929, he or she next saw those prices exactly twenty-five years later, in 1954.
- If an investor bought the S&P in January 1966 or October 1968, he or she did not see the same level on that index until fourteen years later, in August 1982.

The view of many bulls is that a new era of normalcy has arrived in the market which will sustain higher stock prices for some time to come and will forestall any major decline. Let's call it the "This Time It's Different" theology. I'm not a believer. I see a classic financial euphoria around me—a condition for which you can find many echoes through-out history. The minute you hear the justification that "This Time It's Different" and "We never had the combination of so many favourable ingredients to justify further growth," you know we are in the blow-off stage of the bull. These stages can move the market rapidly—look at the incredible years 1995 and 1996. But they are also followed by a collapse which usually brings the market down 30 to 50 per cent. Those who think making money is easy will not sell before the market turns down, and their profits will be wiped out in a matter of weeks. The transition phase from a bull to a bear is a period in which profiting on the long side still *looks* easy, but actually isn't.

The investing public around the world, and North Americans in particular, are having a love affair with stocks and bonds. Trading pieces of paper has become the prime engine of economic activity. Globally, bonds and stocks are now valued at $35 trillion. That is larger than the world gross domestic product. The implication of that number? In an Alice-in-Wonderland turn of events, financial markets have become bigger than the underlying real economy. Since the end of 1994, $4 trillion has been added to the value of stockholdings, and a big part of that is in the hands of households, either directly or through mutual funds. Most of that added value has not been realized: certainly consumer spending doesn't reflect any profit-taking. It remains largely in Wall Street and Bay Street.

Throughout this century, we have witnessed a slow and erratic evolution in the average person's attitude towards equities. They loved them in the go-go 1920s, but the Great Crash and subsequent Depression cured many people of stocks for life. Equities lost 85 to 90 per cent of their pre-Crash values by 1932, the result of a "water torture" of steady and unrelenting decline.

But a new generation in the marketplace and postwar prosperity renewed individuals' confidence. In the mid-1950s, as prices finally made it back up to 1929 levels, Wall Street embarked on a massive campaign to woo back the small investor. Merrill Lynch, in particular, targeted the individual investor living in small-town America by advertising directly to him and by hiring hundreds of stockbrokers to serve him. The result was a doubling in one decade of the number of individuals who owned stocks. The most significant event came in 1958, when rising stock prices pushed the dividend yield below the bond-market yield for the first time since the 1929 crash. That meant that stocks no longer had to pay a premium to investors for the perceived risk of their investment. Individuals at that point came to understand that bonds could only pay a finite return, but stocks had—theoretically anyway—unlimited potential for returns.

The path to our current infatuation took another turn in the 1970s, when the boom times were followed by the wrenching "stagflation" bear of the 1970s. The current generation in the markets is, by and large, unblemished by experience with market pain, however. The yield difference between stocks and bonds has never been greater, and speaks volumes about our attitudes towards equity risk: Where the stock market pays, based on the average dividend yield, a paltry 1.9 per cent, the yield on U.S. Treasury bonds is 6.75 per cent. The stock-mad investor today is piling his and her retirement savings into equities—oblivious or unbelieving of the possibility that stocks can go down, and stay down, as well as go up.

There's an old saying that they don't ring a bell at the top of the stock market. There is also a saying that the guy who rings the bells becomes deaf and can no longer hear them ringing. But do I hear the bells ringing.

The surest indication that the bull market is coming to an end is the fact that it has been too easy to make money in the market. The atmosphere in the last two years is reminiscent of 1929. There is the famous story about Joseph Kennedy, the patriarch of the Kennedy clan, deciding to sell his stocks when shoeshine boys began advising him on what to buy. As Robert Sobel stated, "In 1929, the porter on the Broadway Limited whispered tips on RCA and Anaconda. Today, the waiter at a Manhattan restaurant might very well monitor Micron

Technology's price movements on his pocket quote machine between courses."

So how does the current bull compare with the Roaring '20s, the run-up to the Great Crash of 1929? Strictly speaking, in terms of volume, there is no comparison. There are more investors, small and large, trading a wider variety of issues today than ever before. But there are also similarities. Sobel says that, during the 1920s, a record number of Americans were drawn into stock investments, as they are today. But the preferred purchase for the prudent investor then was bonds. Sobel says old money regarded stocks, and especially industrials, as extremely speculative. If they bought them at all, they generally bought railroad stocks. Of course, in the Crash of '29, rails went south with the rest of the market. In a bear, no equity investment is "safe" from disaster.

But look at it another way. After years of intensive marketing—some would even say propaganda—the investment industry has sold the public on the almost unassailable safety of mutual funds. They are presented as a wise and prudent investment for the ordinary person—much like the old railroad securities.

Most experts in the market today believe the baby-boom generation and its money is fuelling the market's stratospheric climb, and will indefinitely sustain it. The argument goes this way: Aging baby-boomers, who began turning fifty in 1996, have stopped buying Gucci and Cuisinart and started buying Fidelity and Altamira. That explains chronically flagging retail sales and roaring mutual fund sales. Mutual fund marketers have even incorporated demographics into their sales pitches—"The best thing to happen to mutual funds since the baby boom," crowed an ad for CIBC's North American Demographics Fund during the 1997 RRSP selling season.

In a *Time* magazine story headlined "How Much Bull Is Left in the Market?", the magazine declared courageously, "What went up used to come down. But that was before the boomers." In other words, as long as baby-boomers keep pouring their savings into equities, the stock market will continue to rise. Demographically, there are still plenty of boomers who have yet to hit their saving-and-investing prime, so the demand for their favourite investment—equities—will continue to be voracious, driving prices ever higher. Traditional valuations of stocks no longer apply.

Similarly, the June 1995 issue of *Smart Money* ran a piece headlined "Nowhere to Go But Up," the gist of which was the exhortation that individuals should invest in equities before mutual fund managers were forced to drive prices for ever higher. The article quoted one stockbroker as saying, "There are some stocks that should be bought and never sold," which is precisely what bulls were saying in the euphoria of the late 1960s, just ahead of a devastating bear market. The "Nifty Fifty" stocks of the 1960s were known as "one-decision" stocks: You only had to make the decision to buy them since they were so reliable their earnings performance would transcend any economic condition and an investor would never have to sell. The "Nifty Fifty" of that time—companies such as Avon and Xerox—were the darlings of the nascent mutual fund industry. Their valuations ballooned in the bull and, because they were large-cap stocks, they took the major index with them. They were the beneficiaries of a cult of performance that had seized the mutual funds and have astonishing parallels with the temper of investing in today's market. In the 1960s, the bulls argued that "This Time It's Different." Writers Burton Malkiel and Robert Sobel have described the time well, Sobel characterizing the bulls of that period as the "Wunderkinden set of Wall Street"—young, important, with big ideas on investments.

"Although respectful to their elders, they hardly considered any of the antique wisdom of the district worth their while," wrote Sobel. "Rather they would create a new set of rules by which to play the game, and they were supremely confident of success. 'We aim at a 30% growth rate for our clients' assets,' said one money manager in 1965, adding quickly, 'Of course, we expect to do better than that overall, but 30% is rock bottom.' Such a person had never gone through a long bear market and, more importantly, never expected to."

So when I hear a young turk in today's market declaring that some stock should never be sold, it sounds to me like a speculative frenzy rather than a fundamental shift in the stock market paradigm.

There is ample evidence that euphoria is gripping the marketplace.

And present is a psychological context reminiscent of previous stock market bubbles: a wave of mergers and acquisitions, for one. The number of mergers and acquisitions in Canada in 1996 set a record—up 22 per cent from the previous year. Just like the high-flying mid-1980s, corporate executives, such as Microsoft's Bill Gates, and money managers, such as Altamira's Frank Mersch, have emerged as cultural heroes to be admired for their vision and skill. Equities are glorified in the popular press, while countless academic efforts have appeared, aimed at proving the long-run infallibility of equity investing.

We have witnessed IPO fever, mutual-fund mania, and mineral-discovery madness. Amateurs and pros have been fully invested in the market—giant Janus Fund, as an example, was recently at its lowest cash position in years. As with previous speculative orgies, such as that in real estate in the 1980s, people have been buying expensive, overvalued stocks with the intention of selling them at an even higher price to someone else. Or they're holding on to them as a long-term investment, on the assumption that today's levels are permanent. It is unlikely the majority will sell in time to avoid the deluge.

And as with the top of the bull in the late 1960s, people strongly believe in the ability of new technologies to fundamentally change business, and even all of society.

Although the charms of individual sectors have waxed and waned with investors, the market as a whole continues to bewitch investors and confound sceptics. When investors bailed out of high-tech stocks in mid-1996, they moved into blue-chips, and they came roaring back with astounding gains later that year.

Why has the stock market remained so tenaciously bullish? How you answer that question determines whether you are someone who believes that This Time It's Different for the stock market and we are not headed for a crash, or someone who considers history and is convinced that This Time It's Not Different—and that we are still vulnerable to the wrestling match between the bull and the bear.

First, the camp who believe the market is feeding off new sources of energy—and will for the foreseeable future. "New Era Thinking," as it has been called in other speculative booms, is the last refuge of those who must justify stock prices trading at historically high values. In the 1920s, stock buyers said that the United States had reached a new level of permanent prosperity, so the old rules of investing were irrelevant. In the late 1960s, investors reworked their calculations to allow for the new talents of governments and central banks to fine-tune the economy and smooth out the bumps. Before the Crash of 1987, some sages were expecting a wave of Japanese buying of American stocks that would propel the U.S. market to Tokyo-level multiples.

The TTID people these days argue that the rising market is a self-perpetuating marvel. An article in *The Globe & Mail*'s Report on Business in the fall of 1996 illustrated the mindset beautifully: "A crash, though horrific at the time, is not of much importance in 10 years, if you hang on," one broker is quoted as saying. "A number of people say, 'I can't enter into the market.' My reaction is, 'You may have to.' Because interest rates are low and boomers are moving into the investment market like never before."

These are some of the reasons many on Wall Street and Bay Street argue that This Time It's Different:

1. If you've invested prudently in solid equity funds or large, well-established companies, you've got very little to worry about. Even if a market break does occur, a bear is nothing to be afraid of—even for investors in their sixties.
2. History shows that the market always bounces back from a fall.
3. A bear market should be seen as a buying opportunity.
4. Any correction will be short-lived—look at how quickly stocks recovered from the Crash of October 1987.
5. The baby-boom generation is about to buy stocks like there's no tomorrow. Equities will be in hot demand—just as real estate was in the 1980s, when boomers were moving that market.
6. If there is a sell-off, what are the pension funds and mutual funds that dominate the stock market these days going to do with all that cash? (Their cash positions are the lowest in twenty years, at 5 per cent.)
7. The earnings outlook for North American corporations is rosy as

they continue to benefit from the fall of communism and the liber-
alization of economies in Latin America and Asia as enormous
global markets for Western goods are created.
8. Corporations are also reaping the rewards of productivity gains
from technology, which enable faster, cheaper production of goods
and more efficient use of resources.

In early 1994, Ed Yardeni, chief economist for Deutsche Morgan
Grenfell, predicted the Dow would break 5000 by the end of 1995. It
happened earlier than that. In early 1996, Yardeni asked himself, "Is
5000 as good as it gets or do we have a lot more upside potential?" and
promptly predicted the Dow would break 10000 by the year 2000. Aside
from a "refreshing pause" or two, he saw the bull as strong and endur-
ing as long as the economy remained tame, and interest rates stayed
down. "I came to the conclusion that the same secular forces that took
the market to 5000 … could take it up to 10000."

He had four reasons for thinking this. First, the aging baby-
boomers. The Yuppie consumption boom of the 1980s has given way to
slower consumer spending and higher levels of investing in stocks and
bonds. Yardeni argued that, from the 1960s through to the early 1980s,
personal consumption and house prices rose faster than stock prices.
Then, in the early 1980s, all boomers had entered the work force, and
stock prices began rising faster than personal consumption. He compared the S&P 500 to house prices and showed that it fell consistently
in the 1960s and 1970s. But since 1980 stocks have climbed higher than
house prices. In the same way that boomers lifted house prices in the
'80s, they are now inflating stocks. (David Cork, a ScotiaMcLeod broker, had dined out on his prediction that the Toronto Stock Exchange
will hit 17000 by 2010, and all because he believes baby-boomers "will
do to stocks what they did to real estate.")

Almost $60 billion went into equity funds in December 1995 and
January 1996. "It was really just awesome," Yardeni told *Barron's* in
March 1996. "I think it may very well be the beginning of a major shift
by the baby boomers to put even more money into the equity market."

His second allegedly bullish factor is the end of the Cold War, which has dramatically increased—by hundreds of millions of consumers—the global marketplace available to North American manufacturers. It has also made available for the first time new pools of cheap labour. The net effect for multinationals: bigger profits.

The third factor is the belief that high technology has created a fourth aspect of production, in addition to land, capital, and labour: virtually free, real-time information, which gives companies an enormous ability to cut inventory costs, labour costs, and warehousing costs. "You don't need to keep huge warehouses of documents anymore. You can just put them all on optical disk readers and have anybody within the firm domestically or globally access them."

The final secular factor deemed bullish for stocks is downsizing, which he believes will not end. Aside from making some companies more competitive, and therefore more profitable, downsizing has another effect on the stock market: Corporate restructuring has generated enormous cash flow within companies. What was done with that cash? Most companies did not increase their dividend—which is why the dividend yield is so historically low. They have not invested in plants and equipment. Instead, they have been buying up other companies, or, more commonly, buying back their own company's stock. The point of that is to drive up the price of their shares, which pleases shareholders and keeps chief executives employed. "The biggest buyer of stock in the bull market has not been the individual, it's really been the corporate treasurer. And that's the main reason the stock market has moved higher," says Yardeni.

The extent of that has been astounding. Announced stock buy-backs zoomed to $132.4 billion in 1996 in the United States, compared with a paltry $36 billion in 1990; mergers and acquisitions hit $570 billion in 1996, up substantially from about $160 billion in 1990. The number of deals almost doubled in 1996 from the previous year, and almost tripled from 1990. In Canada, such companies as Onex, Inco, Canadian Tire, and all of the Canadian banks (in fact, they were paying top dollar for their own shares as interest rates fell, making financial stocks all the pricier) have embarked on buy-back programs—Inco is enormous, at 55 million shares over five years. In the United States, Chrysler and RJR Nabisco are only two of hundreds.

My reasons Why It's Not:

1. History shows that even solid equity funds and the stocks of large, well-established companies get hammered in a vicious bear market.
2. Yes, stocks always come back … eventually. As Alan Abelson noted at the end of 1996, "The good news is that markets always come back. Or, to be more precise, always have. The least amount of time it took for a post-crash market to get even was seven years. But typically, the investor has had to wait nine to fifteen years before the damage to his portfolio was fully repaired. For today's investor the real prospect is that his portfolio could decline by 56% and stay underwater until 2007."
3. The baby-boomers will put their money wherever it makes sense and, depending on whether there is inflation or deflation, the stock market is not necessarily the right investment vehicle.
4. Institutions will put their money wherever it makes sense, based on their assumptions about the future.
5. The TTID argument depends on low interest rates and low inflation—which are not likely to persist in the long term.

John Brush, founder and president of Columbine Capital Services of Colorado Springs, tested the theory that the stock market is awash with cash from mutual funds, company share repurchases, and mergers and acquisitions, and that is why prices have climbed. Brush calculated that, in the last six months of 1995, equity mutual funds added $74 billion to the Standard & Poor's 500 stock index. Share repurchases added $51 billion, and mergers and acquisitions contributed $89 billion. As a percentage of the capitalization of the S&P 500, the huge numbers represented 1.8, 1.3, and 2.2 per cent, respectively—typical of the previous ten years.

"While pundits are claiming that mutual fund cash inflow from baby boomers is a key reason why things are different this time, our latest research shows this just isn't so," Brush said. He believed the key to the bull's rise is the traditional one: anticipated corporate earnings and short-term interest rates. Expectations of inflation affect stock prices because of the impact they have on corporate earnings and interest rates. Costs, whether interest costs, labour costs, or materials costs, obviously affect future corporate earnings. And as well, a recession is often the result of governments tightening the money supply in order to rein in price increases. That is never good for corporate profits.

So why has the stock market been so tenaciously bullish? The most obvious reason is that inflation, that old demon, has gone missing for some time now. For the past couple of years, no one on Wall Street has considered inflation to be much of a problem. In the United States the rate was 2.7 per cent for 1995, 3.2 per cent for 1996, and 2.9 per cent estimated for 1997. In Canada, it was even lower: 2.1 per cent in 1995, 2 per cent in 1996, and 1.8 to 2 per cent in 1997. In early 1996, a book entitled *The Death of Inflation* even appeared in London bookstores, so obvious was the trend, apparently.

Experience with lower inflation means lower expectations of future inflation. Continuing experience with lower inflation means an even more steadfast belief that inflation has been beaten. With little belief that it will reappear, people expect that interest rates will go low and stay low, and that in turn means longer economic expansions. That, of course, is bullish for stocks.

I am not entirely convinced that inflation is banished from our lives. And there are others who are doubters as well. One is Stephen Roach, Morgan Stanley's economist in New York. He argues that labour militancy—and there has been evidence of that in Canada— and commodities are two potential sources of inflation in the near term. Sherry Cooper, chief economist with Nesbitt Burns, thinks U.S. inflation will stay at 3 per cent in 1997—but only if commodities cool off. John Di Tomasso, who runs the 20/20 Managed Futures Value Fund, which makes bets on commodities by buying and selling options on futures contracts, believes the long bear cycle for commodities that began in the early 1980s is over and that we are three years into a ten- to fifteen-year cycle of increasing commodity prices. Morgan Stanley's Stephen Roach's has been a minority opinion, but he expects an inflation rate of 4 per cent in 1997. If he is right, bear markets in bonds and stocks are a certainty.

But beyond our low-inflation environment, why has the United States in particular, but Canada as well, of late, enjoyed such a remarkable bull run? The answer lies across the Pacific Ocean, in Japan.

In the mid-1990s, Japan was recycling not just its current account surplus, but also much of its savings into the global economy through the U.S. Treasury market. This liquidity infusion was so massive that it had the effect of offsetting global deflationary forces arising from high real interest rates and high rates of unemployment in most industrial countries. The desired effect of this strategy was to restimulate the economies of Japan's best customers for its goods: the G7.

Throughout much of 1996 and late 1995, Japan's net exports of capital were staggering—exceeding those of the world's next four-teen largest capital surplus countries combined. More than three-quarters of the net new issuance of U.S. government debt in the first half of 1996 was purchased by foreigners, and money from Japan was at the front of the flood. The Japanese liquidity gush not only reshaped capital markets in the United States, but also changed the world's economy. The gush of money from the Bank of Japan and the Ministry of Finance has driven the market for long Treasury bonds far ahead of what could have been expected as the Federal Reserve doggedly eased interest rates, triggering rate cuts around the world. Usually, there is a lag between major changes in Fed policy and a response from the economy—at least eighteen months—but, this time, the money pouring into the United States from Japan collapsed the time frame. By mid-1996, the Japanese reliquification began showing results around the world as the torrent of Japanese money moved through short rates to currency, to stocks, and finally into the commercial economy.

Why did Japan do this?

By early 1995, the yen was skyrocketing against the U.S. dollar and had, in effect, become a massive short against the Japanese financial system and its economy. To rescue its parched banks, the Bank of Japan embarked on a plan to drown the financial system in liquidity. The central bank's rates on loans to Japanese banks went down to what one observer called "the science fiction level" of 0.5 per cent. However, that wasn't enough to help the banks recover. By the middle of the year, the usual calm reserve of Japan's powerful Ministry of Finance was collapsing into panic. The result was a bailout styled after that of insolvent savings and loans companies in the United States in the late 1980s. Like the American one, the Japanese rescue plan used taxpayers' money—a first for Japan. The plan was to drive up the beleaguered Tokyo stock market by driving down the value of the yen against the U.S. dollar.

That set off a major rally on the Tokyo Stock Exchange led by the shares of major Japanese exporters like Sony Corp. and Matsushita Electric Industrial Co. Since the Japanese banks have much of their equity tied up in the shares of leading Japanese corporations, they reaped the rewards of the rally.

The Japanese banks have also invested heavily in U.S. Treasury bonds (where the yield is a lot better than the rate they pay for central-bank money). The inflow of Japanese money created a bull market in U.S. bonds and sent the U.S. dollar up (making the Japanese investment even more lucrative). The icing on the cake in all of this is that it has sent U.S. stocks ever higher as well. And without this liquidity, the U.S. economy would be headed into recession by now.

Because Japanese banks calculate their "tier two" equity mainly in the form of unrealized gains on the Japanese stocks they hold, stock-price increases are multiplied six times in capital-ratio calculations. When the Nikkei shot up 37 per cent from the market's bottom of 14295 points through the 20000 level in late 1995, it injected more than a trillion yen into the capital bases of the banks. Similarly, Japanese insurance companies, their books loaded down with worthless stocks and real estate, were allowed to choose either book or market value on exchange rates for the 1996 fiscal year. Finally, the central bank began printing money in earnest. It was, as the eminent stock market observer Donald Coxe of Nesbitt Burns has said, "a banzai attack on deflation."

To make sure the banks caught its drift, the Bank of Japan generously advised banks that it would protect them against exchange losses if they bought U.S. Treasurys in the 100-yen-to-the-dollar range. And at the same time, the central bank made it known that it would maintain the steepest yield curve of any leading industrialized country since the Second World War—an amazing rate of five to six times the banks' cost of funds paid out to their depositors.

It's worth noting that, in 1990, after the new international banking rules went into effect, Federal Reserve chairman Alan Greenspan had tried a similar thing. But he was tight-fisted compared with the Japanese. At the time, American financial institutions were in a similar bind, their capital bases eroded from disastrous real estate investments and other bad calls. Greenspan created a steep yield curve as a way of transfusing U.S. banks with cash, but the best he could achieve was doubling the rate, which helped the American banks only somewhat.

However, in Japan the effect of the strategy was a complete transformation of Japanese and global financial markets. A flood of Japanese investment washed over American and, to a lesser extent, Canadian government bonds. As an example, in July 1995, $32 billion flowed into Treasurys as Japanese banks, insurance companies, and individuals began filling their plates under the new Ministry of Finance rules.

As the yen fell against the U.S. dollar during 1995, and as the steep yield curve kicked in, Japanese banks began earning eleven to twelve times their borrowing cost. As a result of all this: The U.S. dollar shot up 23 per cent and a global bond rally was set off as long-term U.S. Treasurys fell from 6.93 to 5.97 per cent. Long bond rates bottomed in January 1996 and now trade in a range near 6.75 per cent. But sooner or later Japan will have much less money to recycle into the world economy—and a market for U.S. debt will have to be found elsewhere, most likely domestically, at the "right" price.

It won't happen for a while yet for a number of reasons, among them continuing real estate trouble in Japan. The banks still have trillions of yen in losses from the crash in property values. Until they can write that down, the need to reflate will continue, and the risk of inflation in Japan will remain low. The proof that the Japanese banks are still in deep difficulty came in their last fiscal year, when they reported their biggest losses in fifty years, triggered by the writedown of trillions of yen in bad loans. The Japanese economy will continue to need reliquification as unemployment remains high for them and as Japanese companies only now begin downsizing *à la* North America.

Without this wash of cash from the Japanese, the U.S. economy would be headed into recession. Amid the good news of the last couple of years as companies report strong earnings are signs of a slowdown. In the computer and software sector, prices have been falling as growth fades. Stocks of manufacturers of semiconductors and computers have been rising as sales have proved disappointing. The great sell-off in technology stocks in 1996 came at a time when the broad market indices were moving sharply up.

There are other factors pointing to a top in the market. By now it is a bull that has run too high and too fast for too long. Stock prices are high relative to dividends and earnings—and a rising number of companies are reporting less-than-expected earnings, especially, as I've already said, in the sensitive technology sector.

One red flag is that sentiment is moving to an overly optimistic level. This is a classic final stage in a bull market tracking a parabolic incline. Over past couple of years, a number of prominent bears have capitulated to the bullish camp, having lost their credibility as stock prices climbed higher. At the top of the bull in the 1920s, there were few people brave enough to call a bear market amid the euphoria, too. The notable exception was Alexander Dana Noyes, the financial editor of *The New York Times*, who warned of impending doom and was ignored. But his words at the time are worth considering today in the context of extreme optimism in the market. Noyes wrote in September 1929, a month before the Great Crash: "Traders who would formerly have taken the precaution of reducing their commitments just in case a reaction should set in, now feel confident that they can ride out any storm which may develop. But more particularly, the repeated demonstrations which the market has given of its ability to 'come back' with renewed strength after a sharp reaction has engendered a spirit of indifference to all the old time warnings. As to whether this attitude may not sometime itself become a danger signal, Wall Street is not agreed."

In March 1997, the stock markets were panicked at the prospect of interest rate hikes by the U.S. central bank and dropped 10 per cent—

the long-anticipated so-called healthy correction that many market players argued would take enough steam out of the market to forestall a full-bore bear. I believe that the volatility evident in the markets as this book is being written is indeed nothing more than a correction, but that it will not prevent a significant downturn at the end of this year or the start of 1998.

Part of the reason bears—true, committed, got-my-money-out-already bears—have been so scarce on Wall Street and Bay Street recently is that some traditional factors associated with bear markets are not yet present: Money should be very tight; it's not. Inflationary pressure should be building rapidly and continually. There's often a big rise in short-term money rates; that hasn't happened yet—although every time the Federal Reserve deliberates over a rate-setting, everybody holds their breath in anticipation of some bad news. We should see an intemperate growth in the economy—not the Goldilocks economy of late, which is not too hot, not too cold, but just right. Finally, stock prices should be vastly overvalued and, as ridiculous as they seem, by some historical standards they aren't.

The bull's relentless ascent, often in complete contradiction to market and economic signals, trampled a number of well-known bears, some of whom had to invent new reasons why This Time It's Different in order to don their new bull's garb with any dignity. The well-respected Byron Wein, Morgan Stanley's resident bear, recanted in early October 1996 with the report entitled *Wrong on the Big Call.* In April 1996, Wein had called for a 1000-point decline in the Dow, at the time the equivalent of roughly a 20 per cent correction, citing a host of fundamental and technical factors and a slowing of the flow of cash into mutual funds in tandem with a rise in interest rates. Well, that didn't happen.

He was not the only bear to throw in the towel. Elaine Garazelli, who made her reputation when she accurately called the 1987 crash, has been an outspoken bear in 1996, telling her clients to sell everything in the summer, and then again in November. From then until late January 1997, the Dow gained 1200 points, and that is when she reinvented herself as a bull. The day she did that, she shook the New York— and, by extension, Toronto—market because investors and traders considered her a contrary indicator! When she crossed over into the don't-worry-be-happy camp, the Dow fell 100 points.

David Shulman, an analyst with Salomon Brothers in New York, had been calling for a bear market for one year. But in December 1995 he caved in to the pressure of the market and completely reversed his stand. "We are beginning to allow for the possibility that the valuations clocks we have been using are broken; the powerful 1995 rally in stock prices is not a bubble, but rather a signal that the valuation paradigm has changed for the third time in 40 years," he wrote in a report to clients.

The first fundamental shift in stock market valuation was in 1958, when the dividend yield on stocks permanently dropped below corporate bond yields for the first time since 1929 and the price-to-earnings ratio expanded on the belief that governmental policy eliminated the risk of a postwar depression. The mildness of the 1958 recession proved to investors that the risk of a postwar depression had passed. The fear was understandable: following every war since the American Revolution, the United States had suffered an economic depression, with the Great Depression coming eleven years after the First World War.

The second shift was in 1974, when the stock market plummeted and the price-to-earnings ratio collapsed to 7 from 10 as investors learned to their horror that inflation can co-exist with recession. Easy credit and two energy crises in the 1970s triggered double-digit inflation.

Shulman argued that this third shift is the result of continuing low inflation. "The two fundamental fiscal causes of inflation, the welfare state and the warfare state, appear to be in retreat." As a result, significantly higher price-to-earnings ratios can be justified as fair valuation.

The conviction to stay bearish at this time doesn't come easily. It normally comes from having survived quite a few cycles. In the 1970s, the investor was mesmerized by inflation and thus got burned. It took a series of burnings before they all got chased out of hard assets and into paper assets. Now financial assets are the "only" place to be. The short version is that, if valuations mean anything, the good news is all in the stock market.

Despite the elaborate justifications of the TTID crowd, stock valuations look rich to me. And the supply is hardly drying up. When stock prices get high enough, corporate treasurers find a way to issue a lot of paper—just as real estate developers found ways to do condo conversions by the busload when real estate prices got high enough.

When the Dow ploughed through the 7000 mark earlier this year, it was trading at 19.9 times the past year's earnings. Since the Second World War, the U.S. stock market has traded in the range of ten to twenty times earnings, with very few exceptions. Where is the room for higher prices when the outlook for earnings is not nearly as good as it has been in the past couple of years? Extremely vulnerable are the rich blue-chips: Coca-Cola at the time of writing this book traded at forty-four times last year's earnings—63 per cent higher than its multiple two years ago. Microsoft had a price-to-earnings ratio of 52, nearly 80 per cent higher than two years ago.

Valuations of the overall stock market are high, in my opinion, and I see complacency everywhere. In late February 1997, the S&P 500 index was trading at 21 times the previous year's earnings, far above the average of 14.3 times of the past twenty years. The TSE 300 index was trading at 23.2 times, well above its average of 18.9 times in 1996 and 15 times in 1995.

Everyone "knows" cash is trash. In comparison with past market peaks as measured in real terms (1929, 1937, and 1968), this market is hitting a peak. U.S. stock prices are more expensive than they have been at any time in this century. The popular notion that we are in a new investment era is supposed to render invalid such causes for alarm as the lowest yield on the S&P in this century, or that we have gone so long without a significant correction. In truth, there are no new investment eras in the sense that there are no new rules for investment. At most—and this may be the case today—there are only new or different contexts for those centuries-old investment principles. History should teach us that all extremes are eventually corrected by an extreme in the other direction—even though the first extreme is so thoroughly and rationally justified at the time.

Everybody in the 1920s had some sort of theory on why the market wouldn't crash. What everybody thinks is of very little value, especially when it is dished out on financial news shows and newspaper commentaries. However, what is especially of no value is the "analysis" pouring out of every ideas shop: the notion—as prevalent today as it was in the 1920s—that This Time It's Different. Arguments as to why the market can't crash back then ranged from the belief that the U.S. government and the Federal Reserve would not "tolerate" it, to the rationale that the modernization of industry had launched the market into a new and higher valuation orbit.

Today, certain valuation indicators, including the S&P 500 dividend yield, an inflation-based dividend discount model, a trend earnings model, and an hours-worked index, indicate the market is extraordinarily overpriced. Calculations done by one of Wall Street's few bears during 1996 showed that those valuation measures indicated a "fair value" for the S&P 500 in the 400 to 430 range, far below the 600 mark at the start of 1996.

The prestigious *Bank Credit Analyst* concluded that the market, based on its "equity valuation index," a basket of valuation measures related to earnings, dividends, interest rates, and balance sheets, was at an overvalued extreme. In particular, the price-to-dividends and price-to-book value were the richest.

As important as valuations are, they can be way out of line for a long time without breaking the market and they can sometimes be somewhat unreliable. Book values aren't good at measuring the improved efficiency of capital and don't take into account the rising importance of human capital and the move away from machines to high-tech equipment. Currently, dividends are low because of a widespread change in corporate policies. The contemporary corporate belief is that shareholders benefit far more from share buy-back programs than they do from dividends, because dividend income is taxed twice (once at the company and one at the shareholder). Share buy-backs push up the price of a company's stock, thereby giving shareholders a capital gain. What a splendid illustration of today's fervent conviction that bull markets last forever! What has been largely forgotten in all of this is that, in bear markets, dividend-paying corporations usually take less of a stock-price hit.

Over time, the yield or its reciprocal, the cost of $1 in dividends, is probably the most consistent measure of valuation extremes as it represents actual cash paid out. Dividend payouts are cash, which the board of directors must vote to distribute to the owners of the corporation, the shareholders. A high valuation of dividends in the market reflects high expectations for future growth and subsequent payouts. By definition, the true peak is that time when expectations are the highest, not when the actual growth-rate peak is at hand. In 1996, at a 2 per cent yield, investors were paying $50 on the S&P to buy $1 in current dividends—more than they have ever before paid. This was an incredible demonstration of expectations.

Look at the dividend yield for the past 125 years and it's clear that the current yield at 2 per cent is half the long-trend average. Average dividend yields since the beginning of the nineteenth century range from 5.5 per cent in the long span from 1802 to 1992, to 4.2 per cent in the 1966–92 period. So, for almost 200 years, dividends have tended to average 4.5 to 5 per cent.

Dividends are decidedly out of fashion with investors these days, with double-digit capital gains capturing their hearts and minds. But market analysts who have charted the dividend yield over the decades can demonstrate that a long-term investor would have been very successful selling when yields were extraordinarily low, and buying when they were unusually generous. That would have meant selling in 1929, buying in 1932, selling in 1936, buying in 1950, selling in 1973, and buying in 1982.

In a bear market, high dividend–paying stocks usually keep up their price better than those companies paying low dividends. Dividends become very precious when the market turns. In their book *Security Analysis*, Benjamin Graham and David Dodd set out the principles for "value investing," which emphasized that the underlying values of a stock should be reflected in the price, and that return was the single most important element to a stock buyer. That was the basis of the theory that the greater the risk, the greater the reward. Keep in mind this was first posited in 1934, in the aftermath of the Great Crash, when investors had sworn off equities for ever. As a result, corporate bonds yielded more than government bonds, and stocks yielded the most because of their obvious (at the time) risk. In 1950 the dividend yield on the Dow Industrials averaged 6.9 per cent, while triple-A corporate bonds offered 2.7 per cent and long-term government bonds averaged 2.3 per cent. But as that decade wore on and investor aversion to stocks subsided, buyers began to demand issues that offered both capital gain (or "growth") and income.

My friend Ian McAvity likes to say investors should be concerned not only with their return *on* capital, but also with their return *of* capital. When you consider that over time nearly 40 per cent of the total return track record for investing in stocks is derived from dividend payouts and that price appreciation has recently been substantially above the average, while yield has been substantially below average, the message is quite clear. It's known as "regression from the mean," which really means asking the question: How different is today from "normal"? In other words, if you have had several years of stock market returns of 20 and 30 per cent and the average return over the century is 8 per cent, then the conclusion to be drawn is that at some point there will have to be some years of negative or negligible returns in order to stay true to the very long-term average.

The one snag is that value is not all that good as a tool for predicting market moves. In fact, overvalued markets have a tendency to become more overvalued. Rather, valuation is an indicator of how risky a market has become. An overvalued market is more vulnerable because it is less able to shake off surprises such as a rise in interest rates or a drop in earnings or a corporate mishap or a sign of an economic slowdown. The market at this point is relying on sentiment, or how bullish (or bearish) investors feel.

The same mentality was evident in the 1970s, when gold was soaring and people were lining up to buy Krugerrands at $700–$800 a pop, while on the opposite corner others were melting down bowling trophies and wedding silver. The person buying puts blinkers on and says: "I don't want to see the selling because I am buying the big powerful trend." The tricky part is, you can't get a fix on exactly how much will be invested before the trend changes. It was the same when oil kept going up and up. The question became: Which was the marginal barrel of oil—or marginal drop of oil—that was going to put the top on the price? I'm not convinced that anyone can ever answer that.

But it is enough to know what usually comes after that. You know that it's not worth trying to time that one last drop, or that one last up tick in stock prices.

There was a bull trend in place in the Japanese stock market for almost two decades, with an array of powerful forces propelling it forward. People were selling equities door-to-door just like magazine subscriptions. The market was the only place to be. The Japanese were almost exempt from consideration of a bear market. Then, the market simply evaporated. When a market turns, and this is typical of all speculative markets, the key thing is that liquidity disappears.

Sentiment is now the one powerful driver in the market. "Confidence in equities," noted *The Bank Credit Analyst*, "has been boosted by the repeated failure of bearish market forecasts to come true. The failure of gloomy forecasts to come true has forced bearish commentators to adopt increasingly strident and extreme views in order to support their case. However, the pessimistic case is fast running out of arguments. The capitulation or marginalization of the bearish view will set the scene for the euphoria that will inevitably mark the approach of a secular top in the market. The "New Era Thinking " that will justify ridiculous valuations could include the belief that the Fed has learned how to control the business cycle, the view that the budget deficit has been conquered for good and expectations that the corporate sector can continue to boost its share of national income ... Such views will either be misguided or wildly exaggerated but will be used to support increasingly bullish market forecasts.

"The secular bull market will end only when the market is overvalued and investors are fully invested. New era thinking will be rampant ... On the fundamental side, the end of the secular bull market will probably coincide with a drying up of liquidity as well as a deterioration in the macro-economic environment that causes investors to permanently discount a major downward shift in corporate earnings growth."

So what we are looking for is a change in something fundamental and a reason for a cash drain from the market.

On March 8, 1996, the Dow fell by 171 points, the third-largest one-day drop—in terms of points—in the index's sixty-seven-year history. In the Alice-in-Wonderland world of the stock market, it turned out to be merely a blip in the Dow's steady march from the 5000 level on towards the once undreamt-of 7000 mark and beyond. On that day the market shook on news out of the U.S. Department of Labor that employment had been robust, which raised the possibility of an over-heating economy and future wage hikes. The worry was momentary: The next trading day, buyers came roaring back into the market, and the Dow closed *up* 110 points.

Precisely one month later, on April 8, nervous investors once again dumped stocks on the news that employment growth in the United States was twice as strong as had been expected. This time the Dow fell as much as 140 points, but a rally late in the day limited the decline to 88 points. Market players were ho-hum about the volatility, claiming it to be a new paradigm for equity investment. So certain were they of the bull's staying power that one senior trader was quoted as saying: "There's a quiet confidence in this market. No one is afraid. Everyone is just living with this wild volatility." As *The Globe & Mail* noted that day, "Traders who have been around for previous market corrections said there is an eerie faith in stocks right now, compared with widespread nervousness ahead of past corrections. Every drop in stock prices these days represents a buying opportunity."

Along with the stock market, bond markets tumbled wildly on those days, causing the journal *Euromoney* to observe, "There's little discernible logic in a market that drops by the same degree when the Labor Department's monthly employment number is 705,000 new jobs per months as it is when the number is 150,000."

Since 1982, in fact, bonds have behaved remarkably like stocks, selling off sharply on the hint of any sort of news that Main Street would interpret as "good news." It is my belief that what will bring down the stock market are events in the bond market. That is the bull's Achilles' heel.

For several years now, the U.S. bond market has been dominated by foreign buyers. In 1995 alone, they bought $167 billion in Treasurys, well above the amount the U.S. Treasury actually issued: $140 billion.

Central banks and tax havens bought half of that. But much of the buying came from Japanese financial institutions and the Bank of Japan, and it is destined for Washington only as long as it is needed as part of the reflation scheme aimed at transfusing the Japanese financial sector. It is important to keep in mind that no central bank has ever done what the Bank of Japan has been doing since mid-1995, and the impact of this cannot be overemphasized. The Japanese financial system and its economy remain shaky at the time I write this, so the central bank will have to continue to pump money into the system and stay committed to driving the yen down until it sees some improvement in their situation. But it will disappear not only eventually, but overnight, and that is the frightening thing for the stock market.

The third-biggest category of bond buyer has been the trading floors of investment banks. (Many of them are borrowing in Japan at 0.5 per cent interest and making a killing on everything from ten-day Treasury bills to thirty-year Treasury bonds.) This is political, speculative money, which means it is fickle and fleet-footed money. Jim Bianco of Arbor Trading did an analysis of this and explained last year why such widely varying employment numbers can cause similar effects. "When there's so much speculative money, if I'm a trader, it doesn't matter if the number is one job or 100 above consensus, I sell and go short." These are the forces at work in the markets and why an overvalued stock market is so vulnerable. When the bond markets need their domestic buyers back, they will get them, and the equities markets will feel a sudden and huge shock.

CHAPTER THREE

Mutual-Fund Mania

"I've said all along that I don't like the fact that so many
are loaded with stocks or mutual funds and are treating
their holdings as savings. Stocks feel like savings in a bull
market. In a bear market, they feel like the wrath of God."
—RICHARD RUSSELL'S *DOW THEORY LETTERS*, JULY 31, 1996

Just as the 1970s hosted the gold bubble and the 1980s the real estate bubble, this decade—the 1990s—will be known in financial history as the mutual fund bubble.

"Stocks now dominate the net worth of Americans" ran a headline in *The New York Times* in late January 1996, and indeed there has been a major shift in household portfolios towards equities in the 1990s. Last year, stockholdings by Americans totalled $5 trillion, as compared with $4.5 trillion for home equity. So radically has the attitude of the average, middle-class investor with respect to risk and return changed that stocks have replaced homes as the primary nest egg for many North American families. The reach of mutual funds into Canadian households is similarly impressive. In Canada, stocks were the fifth most popular investment in 1989. By 1996, stocks had risen to the number-two place, surpassed only by houses. Thirty-seven per cent of Canadian adults own shares directly or indirectly through mutual funds or pension funds. Whereas in 1993, 2.6 million Canadian households had them, three years later 4 million did.

More than one adult American in three, or more than 40 per cent of American households, now own stock, either directly or indirectly, and the New York Stock Exchange predicts "rapid growth of this figure." Behind these numbers, as *The Wall Street Journal* said recently, "lies a quiet but sweeping transformation, both economically and politically." Individuals now depend on the stock market for a much greater chunk of their wealth and as such have a much stronger personal interest in its welfare. It could be argued that, by extension, they have a stronger affinity for capitalism as well.

Over the past forty years, the stock market has undergone a sea change of enormous scale. Until the 1950s, the individual investor was involved in the stock market directly. By 1995, according to Goldman Sachs of New York, retail investors' direct ownership in stocks (not including participation in mutual funds) had fallen off to 54 per cent. What happened was the institutionalization of equity ownership. In 1949, for example, American institutions owned $11 billion of stocks; by 1971, they held $219 billion, most of them blue-chip, high-cap issues.

Today the dominant players in the stock market are pension funds, mutual funds, and exclusive investment funds for the rich; together they account for most of the trading on any given day. Even with the enormous surge of interest in equities from individuals in recent years—for example, trading on the TSE by retail investors has gone from $26 billion in 1985 to $48 billion ten years later—the institutions' power in the marketplace is profound and mostly behind the scenes, appearing every so often, like a beluga breaking the surface of the ocean, in high-profile corporate takeovers or corporate governance wrangles.

The lemming-like rush to mutual funds has gained velocity over the course of the 1990s. What drives the tremendous inflow of cash into mutual funds is a profound change in the way North Americans are preparing for their retirement: They fear that government pensions will not be there for them, or will be so inadequate as to be non-existent. And where once the vast majority of workers spent their lives with a company anticipating a company pension at the end, now dis-

NAZik

placed, laid-off, spun-off, redundant employees of large companies are finding themselves either with much smaller companies which do not offer defined-benefit pension plans or on their own in entrepreneurial activities and responsible for their own retirement plan. The evidence of this massive change is the rapid growth of "401 (k)" plans in the United States and RRSPs in Canada.

Some observers have argued that the flow of refugees from large corporations to smaller companies or self-employment has had a double-whammy effect in that these freshly minted entrepreneurs—many having gone the IPO route during this bull and many having been remunerated with stock options for the first time—have acquired along with their new careers a vivid understanding and appreciation of the stock market.

Promoted like candy bars with just as sweet an experience implied, mutual funds have emphatically become the preferred method of owning stocks. They've been marketed as simple, easy, and painless money-spinning magic. Consumers haven't needed much persuading, with rock-bottom interest rates driving them out of less risky investments. As for the wary, the mutual fund industry experts have even devised a strategy—"an educational process" where neophytes are "walked through" historical returns on stocks.

The public has made the move from cash to stocks while disregarding the vast difference in risk that the two investment vehicles represent. At the time of the 1990 correction, as little as 25 per cent of household investments were in stocks and mutual funds, while as much as 37 per cent was in cash and money market funds. Even during the market hysteria of pre-Crash 1987, individuals had just over 32 per cent of their assets in stocks. But since 1990, the public has steadily moved from cash to the stock market—so that, by the end of 1995, 41 per cent of household financial assets were in stocks, and 27 per cent in cash and money market funds. In Canada, the breakdown is similar. (At least one study has demonstrated that not a few of these new investors think they are buying insured assets.)

The passion of the "ordinary Joes" for stock market profits is just as evident in other ways. At the nadir of the bear market in the mid-1970s, investment clubs were shutting down—2,000 of them in 1975–76 alone in the United States. Not until 1987 were more clubs formed than dissolved. That year—the year of the October crash—987 clubs sprang up. But the crash scared away the amateur investors, the kind who tend to flock to these clubs, and it was another five years before more than 1,000 new clubs formed in one year. In 1995 that changed radically when more than 5,000 clubs sprang up in the United States as the bull market finally trampled people's fears into the dust. In 1996, according to the National Association of Investors Corp., new investment clubs were forming at the astounding rate of 50 a day.

Another phenomenon of this bull-market bonanza is the large number of people quitting their jobs to play the market full time from their kitchen tables. Some are retirees. But others are like a forty-year-old fellow I know who, having sold his business and based on his "experience" of the last five years of the bull market, is trading his way to retirement paradise.

Today there are more mutual funds than stocks on the stock exchange—well over 7,000 by one count. Mutual fund assets in the United States have gone from $500 billion in 1985 to more than $3 trillion. In Canada, fund assets topped $212 billion at the end of 1996, up from a mere $36 billion six years earlier.

And while bond funds have struggled to keep pace with redemptions, stock funds have exploded in size. Still, stock funds are only one aspect of a gigantic industry that also sells money market funds, bonds, commodities, international investments, and hedge funds of every conceivable sort, from buying coffee to shorting the British pound.

A survey by Royal Trust revealed that in 1996 Canadians put 44 per cent of their RRSP contribution into mutual funds—up from 34 per cent the year before. "What we're seeing," said John Kaszel, director of academic affairs and research for the Investment Funds Institute of Canada, "is the entrenchment of mutual funds as the preferred vehicle and the driving force is the need for alternative investments."

Almost $40 billion was pumped into equity funds in the United States in 1991, and each year since then investors have increased that. In January alone of this year, equity funds attracted a record $29.4 billion from investors—which, on an annualized basis, was higher than the U.S. savings rate, according to the *Capitalist's Companion* newsletter. "Lately, every single savings dollar that households are producing— and then some—is going just into equity mutual funds," the *Companion* declared.

The growth in the past couple of years as the stock market traced that parabolic curve upward has been breathtaking. Fidelity's Magellan Fund today is bigger than the entire equity-fund business was in 1982. Net inflows to stock funds in the years 1993 through 1995 were greater than all the money attracted in the previous sixty years.

To veterans of previous financial binges, this is worrisome. Donald J. Hoppe, an expert on historical cycle analysis, says: "Never before have so many been so wrong about so much. In my 40-plus years of market experience, I have seen a lot of speculative manias come and go, but never anything like the current mutual fund craze."

But who can blame the "maniacs" for their enthusiasm? Over 1996, the Canadian stock market was red hot, and equity funds returned an average 26 per cent—some as much as 60 per cent, and even 90 per cent. No wonder mutual funds attracted a record $41 billion from Canadians in 1996, compared with just $5.2 billion in 1995. (In January 1997 alone, net new sales topped $5 billion.) I sit on the board of directors of O'Donnell Funds, which began operation in January 1996 under the direction of Jim O'Donnell, who was formerly with the Mackenzie group of funds. One year after starting up, the O'Donnell Fund had assets of $1.3 billion and enjoyed the second-highest sales of all fund companies during the 1997 RRSP selling season.

Heading into the annual RRSP selling frenzy earlier this year, consumers were inundated with glossy, feel-good ads with nary a word about risk or markets going down. (Although one mutual fund company, Guardian Group, was brave enough to raise the possibility of a bear market in its ads: "Safety in numbers?" it ran. "Not always." When asked about it, a Guardian senior vice-president explained, "We want to carve out a niche we can come back and defend.")

The accelerating rush into these funds has thus far ensured that a rising stock market is a self-fulfilling prophesy: The behemoth steams steadily uphill as more money chases stocks. "The madness of crowds is abroad in the land," Harry D. Schultz, a stalwart bear told his newsletter fans last year. "Prices are going up because prices are going up. Like the tulips. You don't need good reasons when there's mob rule."

Why the Flood?

In a word, baby-boomers. The dominant species in our society is the baby-boomer and the first of them turned forty-five in 1992. Since then, mutual fund assets have tripled and it's no coincidence. Eighty-four million baby-boomers in North America are beginning to approach retirement—and they are the biggest and longest-lived generation ever. Having done all the acquiring of houses, cars, and toys that they possibly can, they are now more interested in salting money away in financial assets. Investor Economics, a Toronto financial services consulting firm, estimates that individual Canadians will increase their long-term financial holdings—stocks, bonds, mortgages, and mutual funds—to more than $1 trillion over the next ten years, more than double what they held in 1994.

"We are seeing the emergence of a new secular faith," noted my friend Don Coxe of Nesbitt Burns in one of his commentaries. "Baby-boomers have stopped believing in social security and real estate to finance them through a retirement that promises to be long because they work out so vigorously. They have come to believe that stocks are the only investment lifestyle that will let them continue their upscale lifestyles through the next century. They're backing that faith with all the money they can muster."

Fear and greed, as always, are at the root of this mass mania. Like the bull and the bear locked in perpetual struggle, the twin emotional forces of fear and greed animate the investor and dwell within that investor at all times. In every decision to buy or sell a stock, the investor grapples with the fear of not making enough of a return, the fear of losing the profit he or she has made, the fear of being left out of the bonanza as well as the greed of wanting more.

North Americans fear for their jobs; they fear for their retirements—a long stretch of ten or twenty years without enough money. They fear the government pension plans won't be there—indeed, they have been all but told they won't be. (One opinion poll in the United States found that more people under age thirty-five believe in UFOs than believe they will ever receive a social-security cheque.) They worry that inflation will wipe out any pensions they do get. Mostly, though, they quake in the face of the fearmongering served up by the "investment advice industry." The Merrill Lynch Baby Boom Retirement Index warned in July 1994 that "the study's finding that the typical baby-boom household should triple its savings is almost certainly too conservative ... Realistic assumptions about the fiscal outlook for the 21st century imply that the savings crisis is far worse than previously imagined."

That's why they are so receptive to investment advice such as that of York University's Chris Robinson, who told *The Globe & Mail,* "Our research shows that most retirees should invest a significant part of their retirement funds in equity, often 100%. The probability of out-living the money is fairly high for all but those who are quite well off for their age. Women are at much worse risk than men."

Such terrifying news only confirms to middle-class people that they must do everything—anything—to finance their old age. The fear of dying poor outweighs the fear of losing money on the stock market. Giant fund company Fidelity Investments estimates that 70 per cent of all new money coming in is headed into retirement accounts. Essayist Ted Fishman, in *Harper's,* wrote eloquently, "I belong to a generation that not only is hooked on stock investing but also grudgingly embraces speculation as the last best hope against dying penniless."

Which is why so many are financing their flyers on the stock market with credit and why a while back we were treated to the spectacle of the courageous thirty-five-year-old Californian who was buying equity funds on his MasterCard or the blandishments in a recent ad campaign by one of the Big Six Canadian banks to borrow money from it to put into an RRSP.

Take a look at that *New York Times* headline again: "Stocks now dominate the net worth of Americans"—meaning that they held more in common stocks than they held in home equity. Meanwhile, since the early 1970s, personal income has failed to keep up with inflation, and most families have come to rely on two income earners to make ends meet. Not only have Americans and Canadians gone gaga for shares, but they have eaten away at the equity they have in their homes in order to sustain their lifestyles and dive into the stock market, *even while their incomes have fallen and their houses have not appreciated.*

Boomers have committed more than 100 per cent of their net personal savings to equity mutual funds. As the Bessemer Trust newsletter put it in April 1996, "When boomers do something, they do it in a big way, whether it's buying sport utility vehicles or exercise equipment. It would not be a heroic assumption to conclude that they will be any less enthusiastic about their own retirement planning."

Indeed, some advice gurus are actually telling their audiences to remortgage their houses to invest in the stock market, playing on the boomers' fears about eating dog food in their old age. They call it an "adventurous" investment strategy. I call it dangerous. We are in the last leg of this bull, and no one can say how far it will go because we are in the midst of craziness. This sort of thing—telling homeowners to "suck the equity out of your home and play the market"—proves how insane it actually is.

Investor interest in equities becomes pure speculation as more borrowed money is used. And when speculation gets dressed up as prudence, it is a very dangerous game. Speculation is always part of a boom-and-bust cycle.

The near-unanimous verdict from all quarters of the investment game is that only stocks and equity funds will do it for them. Open any financial publication or consult with almost any financial planner and the message is the same. In February 1992 *The Wall Street Journal* ran an article entitled "Why It's Risky Not to Invest More in Stocks." The magazine *Money*, in March 1992, told its readers, "Today, only stocks offer you an excellent shot at double-digit returns. And even with the market at record highs, you don't have to take chances."

The stock market has been sold to consumers as "a one-way street to financial Utopia." Actually, make that an *easy* one-way street, which is what attracted most fundholders to mutual funds in the first place. They don't have to understand price-to-earnings ratios because the expert fund manager looks after that. And plenty have contributions to equity funds deducted straight from their paycheques. "They [meaning investors]," notes Duff Young, senior vice-president in charge of fund research with Midland Walwyn Capital Inc., "don't want to hear any-thing—they just want to write a cheque."

Banks—and who is more prudent than your friendly banker?—now hawk funds over the counter like laundry soap. This was not always so. Canadian banks plunged into the mutual fund business in a big way in the 1990s, as did American banks for the first time, after a concerted lobbying effort on regulators which was prompted, in part, by the exodus of funds from the banks to mutual fund companies.

But of course what has made people receptive to the message of mutual fund purveyors—and what has blinded them to the huge differ-ence in risk between equities and bank deposits—is the vast gulf between stock market returns and what the banks are paying for deposits.

At the time of the 1987 stock market crash, many individual investors dumped their funds and poured huge amounts of money into three-year and five-year GICs (in Canada) and CDs (in the United States). From 1988 to 1990, the base rate for those deposits averaged just over 8 per cent in the United States, peaking above 10 per cent in 1989. By contrast, between 1992 and 1994 the base rate averaged 3.8 per cent. In Canada, the return on a one-year GIC at a major bank was 12.5 per cent in 1990, and 2.5 per cent in 1996.

When those post-crash three-, four-, and five-year certificates came up for renewal, savers suffered sticker shock. They were horrified to dis-cover that their yield was dropping 60 per cent or more. Meanwhile, the "GIC refugee" saw stock markets climbing month after month without a drop. They were mesmerized by the spectacular returns many equity funds were promoting: 20 per cent and 25 per cent annual returns were common. And the indexes were often doing even better: The S&P 500 gained 101 per cent between its 1987 low and year-end 1992. With a fur-ther 16 per cent in dividends added in, the total return was 145 per cent, or an average of 29 per cent a year. Lost in the smoke was the fact that, by the beginning of 1993, the October 1987 crash was finally out of the picture on those five-year track records advertised by the funds. The reminder that markets go down as well as up was gone.

In the headlines, on the talk shows, by the office coffee machine, and at the neighbourhood cocktail party, it seemed everybody was in on the action. Anyone who wasn't was quite clearly a loser or a coward. All of this has conspired to convert thousands upon thousands of conservative savers into risk-oblivious stock speculators.

This is not to say that mutual funds, and especially equity funds, are a bad thing in my opinion. On the contrary, I believe individuals cannot do better *if they are in the stock market* than by participating through mutual funds. Paid professional managers will do a better job of investing in the stock market than most individuals can hope to. The managers have the knowledge and the access to information that an ordinary person does not.

A financial counsellor costs you more money than fund fees and brokers' commissions, but a counsellor will set out objectives according to your desires and will be more responsive to your personal needs. Unfortunately, unless you have enough money to make it rewarding for a counsellor, he or she is not going to have a lot of time for you. It's a variation on the old saw that it's easier to make $10 million than $1 million.

Funds offer ordinary people the chance to get in on all aspects of the market. Arbitrage, value investing, small-cap companies, money markets, specific foreign markets—all of these are available to the small investor, and many of them are offered not just through brokerage firms, but also directly from mutual fund companies, insurance companies, and banks. The competition is intense, not only on performance, but also with regard to convenience. One telephone call allows an individual to transfer funds from one to another, from small-cap to large-cap, from commodities to food, and from sector funds to bonds to equities or money market funds. There's significant competition between load and no-load funds, and on fees and commissions. A careful shopper can get value for money when all is said and done.

I believe the funds are, by and large, well run, well supervised, and well organized to meet the demands of the general public. To date, the institutions have responded well to consumer complaints, and the fees, while not modest, are not outrageous either.

But. Over the long haul, more than two-thirds of money managers are outperformed by the stock indexes. The funds are run by individuals who are just as susceptible to the herd instinct as anyone else. They all tend to follow the bull up—and a bear market down. When you take into account the mammoth size of these funds, however, the gyrations can be truly terrific. Mega-funds like Fidelity, Vanguard, and Alliance can make the market move. When Fidelity's largest fund, Magellan, went into technology stocks, it ended up owning 42 per cent of the sector. Technology stocks shot up. When Magellan subsequently got out of that sector, it alone moved the market down.

People have lapped up mutual funds on the blind belief that they will do as well in the future as they have done in the past. If you buy funds, do so with your eyes wide open to the fact that a fund will go down—almost without exception—when the market goes down, just as it will go up the same way.

People think the diversification offered by mutual funds gives them protection against a market decline. Not so. Funds are not there to take you out of the market when risk occurs. Their job is to keep you in the market; their interest is to be fully invested at all times. Most funds can't and don't sell short, and most can't and don't hold all cash. Obviously, in a bear market, funds will do poorly as a result. The best way to achieve some risk reduction with mutual funds is through dollar-cost averaging—that way, as long as you stick to the plan, you are putting money in at the lows as well as the highs. But that presupposes that you are young enough to be able to ride it out over the long term.

Nobody has the magic formula, and nobody knows what the optimum investment is or what the market is going to do tomorrow. Pouring over the one-, five-, and even ten-year track records of funds is of dubious benefit. Past performance is definitely not a guarantee of future performance. The best an investor can do is know enough to make an educated decision—and, most important, diversify his or her investments.

And in a bear market, the experience of the last fifteen years will count for nothing. The average fund manager has three years' experience. By one estimate, fifty of the new funds started up in 1995 in the United States had managers at the helm who had never run a fund before. The vast majority have never been through the savagery of a secular bear.

I predict that the number of mutual funds in North America will be down by two-thirds by the end of the coming bear market, and many of the mutual fund salespeople will be back teaching school or selling shoes. As with previous cycles, the next bull market will see a new, fresh crop of salespeople who will be unscarred, and thus will be able to give their untarnished optimism and confidence to the market.

Been There, Done That

The concentration of so much money power in the hands of so few fund managers poses a significant threat to the market. But it is not the first time mutual-fund mania has taken hold—nor the first time it will bring down with a high flying bull. Our time is a mirror of previous fund manias. Despite that and the fact that previous manias are well documented and available to anyone as a lesson of history, there are extraordinarily few doubters around today.

In the 1920s, investment trusts proliferated (just as mutual funds have in the 1990s). They and the extraordinary use of leverage were contributing factors to the Crash of '29. It took a quarter-century for investors to believe in the stock market again.

But eventually, growing faith in the long-term allure of stocks expanded during the 1960s as the incredible postwar bull thundered along during that decade, attracting ever-more-eager stock buyers. (In fact, individual shareholders as a percentage of the total U.S. population more than doubled over the course of the 1960s.) Also, that time saw the emergence of what are today the major players in the market— pension funds and mutual funds—as go-go funds, such as Gerry Tsai's fabled Manhattan Fund, entranced a fresh crowd of believers. In the

United States in 1949, institutions owned $11 billion of stocks; by 1971, they held $219 billion in mostly blue-chip, high-cap stocks. But when those funds collapsed or merged, or merely struggled along for years, another generation of investors vowed to stay away from stocks.

Harry D. Schultz, writing in 1964 to an audience thrilled by those go-go stocks and funds, had advice just as applicable to today's investor: "If you had invested $10,000, just 10 years ago, you would now own the state of Wyoming. They don't point out (nor can you blame the salesman for this human tendency to omit what is not appealing) that the last 10 years have been a unique period. There have been 10 years of virtually uninterrupted raging and roaring bull market. It's not likely to *ever* repeat; therefore, to sell funds on the 'hint' it will *probably* repeat is unfortunate."

Each time a mania has grabbed hold of investors, they have seized on the notion that theirs was a new era of stability, growth, and perfectly justifiable valuations. Each time panic was unthinkable as an outcome.

As the end of the bull market of the 1960s drew to a close, such thinking was in abundance. But plenty of funds lost at least 40 per cent of their shareholders' money during the vicious bear market of 1973–74. Eventually those funds came back, but not too many investors were around to see that.

What the Insiders Know

Many of the people behind mutual funds know the truth. On the principle that knowledge is a dangerous thing, some U.S. mutual fund companies have recently begun restricting the information they make public about the flow of money into various types of funds— equities, money market, bonds, etc.—and the flow of money out of funds altogether.

The mantra for today's funds is "Cash is trash and should be spent as quickly as possible." It's most important to remember that the role of a portfolio manager and a mutual fund company is to fully invest the money. They have no choice. Even if fund managers do see a bear market coming towards them, they simply cannot go 50 per cent into cash. There are services which do nothing but measure the performances of various funds, comparing one with another. The individuals who run the funds are under daily scrutiny. If a fund moves from the first quartile to the second quartile, the manager's job is in jeopardy. The competitive pressures are tremendous. And their absolute performance doesn't matter so much as their relative performance—very few concentrate on absolute performance. Robert Marcin, as an example, manages a $2.3-billion fund in New York called MAS Funds Value Portfolio. At the end of last year, as the Dow paddled above 6500, he outlined his strategy for the fund: he was "bending" his usual investment rules to pump up the fund's stockholdings, he said, and he was slower to sell issues that had risen sharply. As new money poured into the fund each day, he was investing it as fast as he could.

Meanwhile, in his personal portfolio he had cut back on his own stockholdings and was planning to put some of his money into call options, limiting his risk in a market decline—the same market he was rushing headlong into for his clients.

Marcin couldn't manage money in the office the way he was at home because mutual fund investors have demanded rampaging bullishness. Fund investors are quick to penalize fund managers who demonstrate mere caution, never mind outright bearishness—and keeping even 10 per cent of a fund in cash can drag down the performance numbers that investors monitor so closely.

Look at what happened to Jeffrey Vinik, the man at the helm of Fidelity's $55-billion Magellan Fund. In May 1996, Vinik suddenly departed Magellan. The publicly presented reason for this was that, as manager of the world's largest fund, he was tired of operating in the spotlight and wanted to start his own investment company. But the real reason was his decision to take one-fifth of the mammoth fund out of high-growth technology stocks and sock the money away in bonds and cash. Vinik had grown cautious at the close of 1995, believing that the U.S. economy was about to slow down. He had also grown wary of stock valuations. "In the past, such high levels of optimism have been a good reason to be somewhat cautious in terms of the stock market," he said at the time. "History shows that when investors have poured into one area of the financial markets—be it gold and oil in the late 1970s, real estate in the 1980s or perhaps stocks today—future returns in that area tended to be dampened."

The trouble was that the high-tech stocks had been powering Magellan's high-test performance. And Vinik's defensive strategy drove investors and their $500 million away from Magellan and into the arms of its competitors in one month alone, as bond prices in fact fell and the economy steamed along. For the first five months of 1996, Magellan had a gain of 3.5 per cent compared with the 8.1 per cent increase for the S&P 500 index (including reinvested dividends).

When the market finally does break, investors should remember this story. It is they who comb the mutual fund rankings and switch funds as often as they change shirts, looking for ever-more-spectacular returns. As the sagacious Alan Abelson wrote at the time, "For the message Vinik's fate broadcasts to the pampered legions of mutual-fund money managers is powerfully direct: Caution is death. Each and every one, in effect, is importuned to gaze on Jeff Vinik and reflect: There, but for the grace of being fully invested, go I!"

The Big Question

For some time, the bull has had the wind at his back: Rising stock prices attract fresh money into mutual funds, which then chase stocks, causing their prices to rise further—which only attracts more new money to the market. A seemingly virtuous circle. In particular, the twenty-five biggest companies on the New York Stock Exchange—such names as Coca-Cola and General Electric—account for almost 33 per cent of the value of the S&P index. They lead the market in size and in performance—outperforming the index as a whole, as measured by return, by twice as much. Recently, investors have fallen in love with index funds, which have vastly outperformed the actively managed funds. The growth of index funds has been the story of the market in the last two years. As those funds grow, they bid up the prices of the large-cap stocks that dominate the index; the rise in the big-cap stocks attracts more investors' cash to the index funds, and on and on it goes.

When something—it could be anything—eventually triggers a fall in stock prices, those and all other types of mutual funds will spring a leak and that same money will gush out of them just as torrentially as it poured in—causing stock prices to fall further. A vicious circle.

The people who stand to get hurt the worst by the coming bear market are the people who bought mutual funds at top prices during the last couple of years. And 80 per cent of all the money invested in mutual funds has come in since the 1990 low. These people weren't in the market for the 1987 crash and didn't experience the downturn in 1990, when the TSE hit bottom at 3009 points and the average equity fund lost 10 per cent of its value.

Newsletter publisher Richard Band colourfully calls what he sees as an impending mutual fund meltdown "The Panic of the Bear Market Virgins." How much pain tolerance does this group have? That is one great unknowable.

The other is how the fund managers will react. The vast majority of portfolio managers are young and untested in a bear market. What they know about bears they've read in history books, if that. Not only that, it's not their money at stake. Either they haven't got a dime in their own funds or, like Robert Marcin, they're doing something completely different with their personal portfolio.

The line from the fund industry is that investors will remain calm and stay put because they are in the market for the long haul. "I have a lot of trouble with doomsayers who think there will be a run on mutual funds. There has never been, in my experience, much of a rush on redemptions," Keith Douglas, a former head of the Investment Funds Institute of Canada, has been quoted as saying. "If you understand that investing is a long-term undertaking, you'll be thankful you're getting your funds when prices are a better deal."

This, of course, is the old buy-on-the-dips theory. And in short, snappy downdrafts, it has proved a good one. In June and July 1996, when high-tech and junior mining stocks plummeted, loyal investors were subsequently rewarded for staying in when most of those stocks recovered nicely.

However, I am not talking about a short period of pain. Experts confess they have no idea how long come-lately mutual fund investors will stick it out as the market heads drearily downward. I agree with the comment of an investment consultant who was quoted as saying, "Baby-boomers tend to move in a herd, a massive herd. They don't know what risk-taking is. They only know the return side of the equation." And when boomers find themselves choosing between a GIC paying 5 per cent or an equity fund losing 10 per cent, they will in all likelihood make the same decision en masse (as they have done about everything from blue jeans to houses) and head for the exits.

When fund industry people say that historically investors haven't departed mutual funds in droves during a downturn, they are right. What they don't say is that they move their money out of equity funds into bond or money market funds.

At the end of the 1970s, following ten years of slump and decline, mutual fund assets had drained from the stock market to the money market. Where once equities had made up 80 per cent of assets, in 1979 that had slipped to less than 50 per cent. Mutual fund managers were of the opinion that, as one at the time put it, "it would take a sustained bull market for a couple of years to attract broad-based investor interest and restore confidence."

He was right. But the effect of that switch wasn't so much on the fund industry—although there was a major contraction there—as on the stock market, where fewer buyers always means lower prices.

The question today of what these neophytes will do is of such consuming interest for the fund industry that inflows and outflows to mutual funds are now monitored on a weekly basis. Previously, monthly tracking of sales and redemptions was good enough.

The industry knows that stock prices can rise only as long as demand outstrips supply. Mutual fund buyers have played an enormous part in creating the mania for stocks in the last few years. Their presence in the market in the next few will determine just how bad the market break is. We got a taste of what will happen in March 1997, when stock markets fell 10 per cent and mutual funds experienced net redemptions overnight. In the United States, where funds have much less cash on hand compared with Canadian funds, fund managers have very little room to manoeuvre when unitholders start bailing out.

Those who buy last tend to sell first. I expect that a prolonged faltering market will produce a sudden rush of redemptions. Fund managers will have to dump stockholdings in order to pay off departing investors. It will be that much more difficult to sell shareholdings in a falling market.

The one kernel of hope lies with the possibility—not, I might add, probability—of "long-term," regularly contributing investors sticking with their equity funds. Their cash inflows would help fund managers redeem the unitholders cashing in without having to sell stocks. Even more important, a steady flow of incoming money would allow fund managers to buy stocks at a cheaper price—and create a market that presumably would staunch the bloodbath.

Most of the novice investors who have flocked to mutual funds have displayed market timing typical of their group: in 1988 equity fund managers faced a flow of money out of their funds as individuals licked their wounds from the October 1987 crash. Month after month there was a net outflow. Yet during this time, the stock market actually went up. In fact, the value of the U.S. stock market was about a third of what it is today.

A few years ago, *Forbes* looked at the market timing of small investors and concluded that it was so spectacularly bad you could almost use it as a contrary indicator. In the late 1970s and early 1980s, as the bear market came to an end, retail investors were continuing to cash in their stocks. Well after the current bull got under way, they started buying again—just as the market took a brief turn down in late 1983. The following year, as the market rebounded, they were, of course, selling. Then, over the summer of 1987, ordinary folks were the most enthusiastic of stock buyers. That is, until the crash in October.

That crash taught many people *not* to pull out of their equity funds. The brevity of the collapse demonstrated to amateurs that it was those who panicked and called their brokers who lost their money. Those who braved the turmoil made all their money back and more. So these investors have had the experience of a sharp, sudden, quickly reversed market break. What they have not yet had a taste of is a slow, grinding drop of ten or twenty points a day for months and months, and maybe years.

Securities regulators are bracing themselves for the fallout that will inevitably come when these novice stockholders—the archetypal little guys of the 1990s—confront their first bear market. On both sides of the border there is a move afoot to have mutual fund companies explicitly warn investors that there are bear markets as well as bulls. "There is a whole universe of investors out there who have never been tested— whose only experience has been a bull market," Arthur Levitt, the chair of the Securities and Exchange Commission, noted in spring 1996.

It takes an incredible amount of money to keep a $7-trillion universe of capitalization afloat. The stock market has never before experienced such a flow of cash, and its dependency on it makes it extremely vulnerable. The higher the market, the more it takes to keep it powering upward. Six years ago it took about $1.3 billion in fresh funds to raise the major U.S. averages 1 per cent. It now takes more than $4 billion to accomplish the same feat.

What will happen when interest rates rise and the "GIC refugees" flee back to their natural habitat, the money market? And what will happen when the baby-boomers, who have financed all aspects of their lives (including their savings) with debt, finally face their day of reckoning? What will the market do if the mutual fund flow slows to $8 billion or $10 billion a month—a relative trickle compared with the bonanza of recent years?

A couple of years back, at an investment conference held by *Grant's Interest Rate Observer*, Jim Bianco of Arbor Trading, in noting that 80 per cent of the money in mutual funds has come in since the 1990 low and that that money has not experienced a 10 per cent correction, said, "If you can tell me what gets us down 10% in the stock market"—in other words, what would trigger a correction—"I can tell you what gets us the next 20% after that!" Meaning those easily frightened investors who are most likely to sell into serious market weakness once a significant decline is under way, even though they will deny this and claim to be in for the long term right up until the moment of fear strikes. It is emotionally a lot "easier" to buy high and sell low. Indeed, that is what the majority of investors do at major turning points in the market, and it is emotionally easier to follow what the crowd is doing.

Small-time investors have amply demonstrated their predilections in the past. They bought bond funds at hefty prices in 1993 and sold them in despair one year later—into a falling market which then recovered. Others bought international or emerging markets funds when they were already up 50 to 60 per cent several years ago and sold them in a panic at much lower prices when Mexico hit bad turbulence at the end of 1994.

The Financial Times notes that, in Japan, equity mutual fund assets were $350 billion at the start of 1990. Japan's total today has plunged to about $30 billion, or a minuscule 2 per cent of the U.S. equity mutual fund assets. More than six years of –8 per cent compounded returns has driven sufficient numbers of investors away that total assets in yen have shrunk by more than 91 per cent. And despite short-term interest rates in Japan that are as close to zero as you can get, it could be a generation before the Japanese have enough confidence to return to the stock market.

Then there is this parallel closer to home from 1964: "It was often said prior to the 1962 crash"—actually as things turned out it was a correction, and the big bear of the 1960s wasn't until the end of the decade—"that one of the reasons we couldn't have a crash is that the mutual funds would act as a great bulwark, a stabilizing force. They would be in there scooping up bargains, or, even if not buying, at least not selling because they are long-term holders," wrote Harry D. Schultz. "The 1962 crash has already saved us the trouble of repeating what I have been saying privately for several years—that mutual funds will not be able to stem any selling tide." That was precisely the case in 1929. In *The Great Crash*, John Kenneth Galbraith points out that "it was evident the investment trusts, once considered a buttress of the high plateau and a built-in defense against collapse, were really a profound source of weakness."

At the time of the sharp market sell-off in June and July 1996, the flow of money into U.S. equity mutual funds dropped $3.5 billion compared with an average $18 billion a month over the past year. It was the same thing in Canada, where mutual fund enthusiasts sent an even $1 billion into stock funds in July, down from the average monthly $1.7 billion for the previous six months. The question at the time was which came first: the market downturn turning off investors, or turned-off investors withholding some of that tidal wave of cash that had been feeding the market frenzy—thereby causing the market to drop as fund managers stopped buying stocks?

"When the bubble bursts it will hurt us all," says Schultz, who has seen a bear or two. "The savings of this generation could easily be slashed by at least 50%. It could be even worse." Once the exodus begins, the doors won't be wide enough to accommodate even a fraction of those trying to get out. The fund companies already know this. Behind the scenes some of them are quietly arranging credit lines with banks to borrow millions in the event of a crash. Millions in a multi-billion industry? How effective will that prove? Besides which, it actually serves to margin the mutual funds—at a time when stock exchanges are already reporting record levels of margin debt.

"The acid test of any bubble," said *The Richebacher Letter* in late 1995, "is the relationship between available savings and the total flow of funds into the market. The money pouring into U.S. markets comes from various sources, but least of all from genuine savings. Most of it arises from two extraordinary sources: a race out of money into securities, and protracted credit creation vastly in excess of current income and GNP. The first makes for a money bubble, the other one for a credit bubble. Every bubble is vulnerable to money tightening."

My belief is that the great bull run of the 1990s will come to a crashing halt as the supports propping it up crumble from the sheer weight of a 7500 or 8000 Dow. What remains to be seen is whether a normal market break becomes a mega-crash. If millions of novice fund investors panic, they will trigger an avalanche of selling not seen before.

The equity fund industry likes to talk about how tiny net redemptions are in terms of a percentage of its net assets. But, since 1990, the funds' share of total market capitalization has soared from an average of 7 per cent in previous bull markets to the current 21 per cent. The "tiny percentage" translates into an enormous amount of money—by one calculation the equivalent, in a crash like October 1987, of $52 billion in net redemptions in one month in the United States.

And it will not stop there.

When the innocence of today's mutual fund investor is shattered by the reality of a severe bear market, you can bet the fund industry itself will not escape unscathed. When the bear of 1973–74 nearly halved the Dow index, it permanently changed the way people viewed investment performance. Before the jolt, individuals and institutions really weren't measuring the returns of their money managers. But when these professional managers, with their portfolios packed with "Nifty Fifty" growth stocks, saw prices tumble 54 per cent, they lost their image of invincibility. From then on, investors began holding them to closer scrutiny—comparing them against each other and the indexes.

The economy will also feel the sting of the bear. In 1984, economists from Wharton Business School and Harvard demonstrated that share-owning consumers were far more likely to shift their spending patterns in response to stock market gyrations than those who did not own shares. That was true when about 28 per cent of households owned stocks. With share-ownership now at the 40 per cent level, imagine the impact of a bear market on Main Street as consumption evaporates.

The enormous amount of household wealth now tied up in equity markets, rather than tucked away in bank deposits or other traditionally safe harbours, means that not only the stock market, but also the economy, will suffer as huge amounts of wealth are wiped out. Most especially, the banks, which have eagerly extended record amounts of credit-card and household loans over the course of the bull, will be highly vulnerable in a major market break.

CHAPTER FOUR

Market Moves

"Psychology can turn overnight like a key in a lock.
Click—the party's over."
—AN OVER-THE-COUNTER BROKER IN NEW YORK ON THE
EVE OF THE BEAR MARKET OF 1969

The stock market has been in retreat one-third of the time during this century, and yet there is a bear market even in information on bear markets. Very little has been written about them. And no wonder: There is not much fun and not much money to be made when stock markets are headed south. After all, the basic premise of the stock market is profit, and that necessarily implies a rising market and a general feeling of promise, hope, and optimism. It is worth noting that, at the height of the bull market in 1987, the Chicago Board of Trade found it had a traffic problem in its Treasury bond pit, so it installed turnstiles at the door: two to get in and one to get out.

In a bear, the fundamental objective is much less dynamic than profit-seeking. It is simply to preserve what wealth you have acquired: not to lose it, to keep it out of harm's way. This is hardly a glamorous concept, and so it is not surprising that the library shelves are filled with how-to rather than how-not-to books.

However, in the next few years, I guarantee you, there will be plenty of people searching for advice on the new market environment.

It is instructive to browse through the financial magazines and newspapers published during past bear markets. Even in a long bear, such as the one lasting from 1969 to 1974, the periodicals published at the time are full of optimism. There is talk about the last rally, the current rally, the coming rally. Or the stock guaranteed to buck the downward trend. The focus of most investors during a bear remains unchanged even as the markets slide. Columnists and so-called experts seem to have blinkers on: they focus on what is happening week to week, and what stocks are a buy, and the encouraging news that is surely an indication of better things to come in the short term. They miss the big picture. They fail to see where they are in the long-term cycles that determine the overall direction of the market.

The vast majority of investors have never experienced the pain of a bear market. They are baby-boomers and older and they were age thirty during the last severe bear in the stock market. At the time, they couldn't have cared less. The same goes for the vast majority of brokers currently working in the business.

But, whether they realize it or not, they have felt the sting of the bear in other markets.

Say you bought your home in Toronto or Los Angeles in 1988—pretty well at the height of the property bubble. You paid $500,000 for it, having enthusiastically outbid two other eager buyers. At the time, you were moving up in the real estate market because, in your experience, you could only win with real estate. Nothing else could compare with it as an investment. The prices of houses in your city had tripled during the 1980s, and most people had—on paper at least—vastly increased their net worth as a result. A few years later, you wanted to sell your home, for whatever reason. Much to your surprise, real estate agents told you prices had fallen by 25 per cent. Not only that, the volume of house sales was down 40 per cent; there were fewer buyers out there willing to pay any price, never mind the price you wanted. You decided not to sell—you don't want to take that kind of a hit on your investment. You wait because the market has to improve—it always does in real estate.

Now it is seven years after you bought your half-million-dollar house. Now you really do have to sell because you are relocating or divorcing or trying to raise capital for a new business. You discover prices are now down a full 45 per cent, although volume has begun to creep back up a bit from its low point. Dispiritedly, you put your house on the market because real estate agents tell you the residential market is not coming back for at least five more years. It sells—for $300,000, eating into most of your equity. You have just experienced a bear market.

Not only that, you have just behaved the way most people do in a bear: resisting the idea of selling after the peak, and eventually selling in despair when the market is about to turn.

So what is a bear market? In simple terms, a depressed or declining market. Falling markets of any kind are caused by supply exceeding demand. The supply of money chasing stocks can dry up for a number of reasons. When interest rates rise, other investments, such as GICs, become more attractive and siphon off those investors looking to minimize their risk. Sometimes there are structural reasons affecting supply and demand: as baby-boomers age and stop buying big homes and fancy clothes, they start saving and investing for their retirement, flooding investment markets rather than consumer markets with their cash. (Hence, what happened in real estate and retailing during the past few years.) Or something else can tip the balance: in a bullish market issuers try to catch the wave up with new issues, but too many can swamp a market, drowning demand and stalling price momentum.

People in the stock market tend to think of it and describe it in anthropomorphic terms. The market has a will of its own and is said to be "looking for direction" or "trying to rally." Similarly, bear and bull markets take on the characteristics of their namesake beasts. A bull market charges ahead; a bear market is treacherous, and investors feel the sting of its claws. Stock market terminology abounds with overly precious names and euphemisms for bears, most of them an attempt to describe the vast variance in the degree and duration of bear markets. There are mama, papa, and baby bears. There are dramatic bear markets that feature crashes, meltdowns, and collapses on the order of 30 to 50 per cent. There are market breaks, and more sedate "corrections" of 10 per cent. There are mild downturns of mere single-digit proportions. Then, there are bull markets that simply turn bearish and go side-ways for a long, long time, as stocks did in the 1940s.

As with bull markets, bears can be cyclical or secular. The long-term secular bulls and bears cut wide swaths across this century. The current bull stretching from 1982 to today is most definitely a secular beast, as was the postwar bull running from 1948 to 1966. Within those broad upward and downward slopes in the market are cyclical turns of events. Most of them have been short and mild episodes. But the market's history is punctuated by gut-wrenching panics. The infamous Panic of 1907 saw the market in free-fall for four months, dropping 45 per cent, before the famous financier J.P. Morgan mounted a campaign to rescue a failing trust company and rally bullishness on Wall Street.

Bears are also as common as the cold. During this bull market alone, there have been a number of bears of varying ferocity, including the lightning-quick 1987 crash, when the Dow fell 36 per cent over fifty-five days, and the 1990 slide, when the Dow had 21 per cent knocked off it in four months and the TSE saw 23 per cent drop away over a twelve-month period.

Over the course of this century, a third of the time the market has been in retreat. As Ned Davis Research, of Nokomis, Florida, discovered when looking at all declines in the Dow Jones Industrial Average of 5 per cent or more for *The Wall Street Journal:* Since 1900 there have been 318 such declines, an average of 3 a year. Routine.

Ian McAvity, who writes the newsletter *Deliberations,* looked at the S&P 500 going back 124 years to 1871 and tracked up trends and down trends, using monthly averages. He considered a trend upward if prices advanced more than 15 per cent, downward if prices fell more than 13 per cent. In that 124 years, the market was in decline 37 per cent of the time. Since 1990, there have been zero declines of more than 10 per cent. This is obviously a huge variance from the mean. No wonder modern investors can't believe a bear market is for real.

Thirty years ago, bear-market expert Harry D. Schultz calculated the same thing: Over one third of the time the stock market was drop-ping. "When you consider that the depressed psychological climate at bear market bottoms prevents the majority from investing at the same time, it means by the time they recognize a bull market is present, it is half gone." That, he concluded, "should explode the myth that you can just invest and sit and wait, ignoring bear markets."

Much academic effort has gone into studying the stock market. To my mind it is cyclical, like so many things in life, from economic prosperity to grasshopper plagues. Name it and there is a theory to explain how the market moves in tandem with something: U.S. presidential terms, years ending in the number 6, hemlines. Russian economist Nikolai Kondratieff, working in the 1930s, devised a repetitive pattern of financial and economic behaviour based on a fifty-four-year cycle that has stood up remarkably well. It is really long term. The bottom of the Kondratieff cycle was in 1932, which means that beyond the coming bear market there is real upside opportunity for stock investors. (As with all cycles, within a long-term up or down trend, there are always smaller up and down ticks. No cycle is straight up or straight down.)

There have been many attempts to quantify, rationalize, and make science out of the stock market. I rely on two particular theories in determining my investment strategies.

One is the Elliott Wave theory, especially as interpreted by Robert Prechter, Jr. and Peter DeSario. I listen to them regularly and formulate my trading strategies based on their analyses. The principles of the Elliott Wave are good when applied to index futures trading, but they are also valuable with equities. DeSario provides a daily fax service of his own on the technical condition of the major futures markets. But previously he worked with Prechter and was editor of *The Elliott Wave Forecast* for a number of years

Elliott Wave theorists have been predicting a vicious bear for some time. In 1995, Prechter told his readers that a number of indicators pointed to an impending crash of epic proportion. He also predicted a devastating economic depression to follow.

(Perhaps this is a good time to point out that not every market break precedes a recession but every recession has been preceded by a market break. The market generally moves about six months ahead of the economic cycle. In this way, the market is a barometer rather than a thermometer: it is anticipatory, telling of coming economic weather, not what is happening outside on Main Street at that moment.)

Prechter's analysis showed that the market in the winter of 1996 was engaged in a "blow-off," that is, an accelerating upward move that resolves itself in a crash. A blow-off is a rare event. According to Prechter one has not occurred in modern history in stocks, although they are common in the commodities markets. Indeed, the last time the stock market had a commodity-like ending was in 1720, when the investment manias sweeping England and France came to a convulsive end.

The Elliott Wave theory is based on the principle that markets behave in a certain way based on cycles of five. Mass-investor psychology swings from pessimism to optimism and back in a natural sequence, creating specific patterns of stock-price movement. Each pattern, in turn, has implications for the market in terms of its progression, past, present, and future.

It is rooted in a mathematics construct devised by a famous thirteenth-century mathematician named Leonardo of Pisa, better known by his nickname, Fibonacci. Ralph N. Elliott, a globetrotting accountant working in the 1930s, took Fibonacci's work and applied it to movement of the stock market. He assumed that the simplest description of a bear market is a straight line down—one wave—and the simplest description of a bull market is a straight line up. Elliott found that bear markets most often subdivide into three waves: down, up, down. Bull markets subdivide into five up-and-down waves. It takes one complete bear market and one bull to make a cycle.

Prechter takes Elliott's work one step further when he theorizes that the stock market is a direct reflection of mass psychological change. "The market averages are one of the greatest manifestations of mass psychology in the world," he says. "Collective psychology is impulsive, self-generating, self-sustaining and self-reversing. The dynamics of social psychology operate by the same dynamics over and over again, regardless of different attendant historical or cultural specifics. Events that make history are the result of mass mental states that take time to develop. This is the only possible explanation for the constancy of structure and consistency of pattern that markets reveal."

Prechter argues that the current bull market is the fifth wave of a "Grand Supercycle" (you could think of it as the Mother of All Market Cycles) and that it has been around for the better part of most people's lives. Such a wave is characterized by a market that attracts new and unsophisticated players who have been watching the bull on the sidelines for years and finally become convinced that they should play. For that reason, the market, or large segments of it, become highly overvalued. These new players have no concept of value and are willing to buy simply because they believe someone else will be along to buy their stocks tomorrow. In Prechter's scenario—which echoes other work done on euphorias—the whole thing ends up in a speculative bubble, "a chasing of paper value for quick profit." Prechter believes that this fifth-wave bull market has been helped along in its euphoria by the development of the highly leveraged stock index futures market and the options market, and by increased media coverage of financial news.

The bottom line with Prechter is that he is calling for a major bear market. He sees stock prices taking their biggest fall since 1929–32, with the average stock dropping 90 per cent in value. As for the economy, he says, "The late 1990s and early 2000s will be depression years."

I disagree with Prechter on two counts: the timing of the bear and its severity. However, I obviously do believe he is right in forecasting a major bear market. Prechter defended himself in 1995, when it became obvious his original call was wrong: "The really important thing is not to be right all the time on every detail, which is impossible, but to understand the big picture, to recognize the grand design behind the apparent randomness of human behaviours and indeed behind the whole course of history. A long time ago, I wrote that this long wave plateau bull market would not end until all wave and cycle analysts were totally discredited. At that time, I surely did not realize how literally true that prediction would become or how long it would take. Even in 1929, there were still a few prominent bears and skeptics [like the aforementioned Alfred Dana Noyes, financial editor of *The New York Times*] who did not succumb to the 'New Era' delusion. Now, however, there is no one at all in the mainstream financial establishment who is sounding the alarm or who even urges caution. I do not regret leaving the party before the grand finale."

But why have faith in someone who has been wrong for so long in his timing? Richard Russell, in his *Dow Theory Letters* in October 1996, dealt with that question this way: "I always watch a brilliant analyst who's been wrong over a period of time—he's close to being right (although, ironically, he'll also be disbelieved)."

The other theory to which I subscribe in looking at movement in the market is the Dow Theory. It is the granddaddy of market theories, first articulated at the turn of the century by Charles Dow, founding editor of *The Wall Street Journal* and inventor of the famous New York stock index. He believed that stock-price patterns recurred, and the theory attempted to forecast the market based on the link between market cycles and business cycles. Dow's writings have since been elaborated upon by a series of theoreticians including Robert Rhea, who, some people argue, have distorted Dow's original observations of market cycles by creating intricate methods of predicting future stock-price movements based on current trends.

I am aware that this theory has lost much of its credibility and that technical analysis itself is under attack in some quarters because stock-chart reading ignores the notion of "value" in the market. And there are those who argue that today's rapid dissemination of information— to wit, the Department of Commerce releases statistics and the market instantly reacts—has rendered Dow's four-year cycles outdated.

But for we believers, the Dow Theory provides a means of detecting a bear market. In simple terms, this is how it works: If the Dow Jones Industrial Average reaches a new high, sells off a significant amount, rallies but does not make the previous high, and then turns down again, breaking the previous low, then it is a good bet that a bear market has begun. It is important to have "confirmation" in the form of similar performance in the Dow Jones Transportation Index. The break below the previous low should be reasonably decisive, and on appropriate volume as well.

Let's look at last year as an example. On May 22, the Dow Industrials hit a closing high of 5778. Two months later, on July 23, they hit a correction low of 5346.73. On May 22, the Transportation Index hit a high of 2296.20, and a low of 1965.73 on July 24. At that point, according to the Dow Theory, a bull market would be reconfirmed if both averages broke their May highs. On the other hand, if the two indices break through the previous lows, it signals a bear market. Sure enough, on September 13, 1996, the Dow Industrials broke through the previous high and went on to set new records, including, not long after, smashing through the 7000 mark. The Transports broke through their previous high on December 3, 1996.

No matter what yardstick is used, the question for market-watchers is the same: What moves the market? It is a question both central to success in the market and maddeningly difficult to answer. It has been the pursuit of market analysts for as long as there has been a stock market. And there are two schools of thought: the market is a reflection of mass-investor psychology, or the market reflects intrinsic values.

The two styles of market analysis developed during this century as the New York stock market developed in size and influence. Late in the last century and leading up to the Great Crash, the stock market was more like a casino or a race track, manipulated by powerful behind-the-scenes players who worked in concert to manipulate stock prices. As business historian Robert Sobel has written, "If there was anything close to a market theory, it was that a company was worth the net value of its visible assets. Any amount that its stock price rose above that level was somehow illegitimate."

That changed, however, with the work of Dow, who sought a rational explanation for stock market behaviour. He decided that daily changes in the market's direction were the result of speculators, that short-term changes—over the course of a few weeks or months—reflected the activities of large investment pools, but that longer-term market moves of roughly four years were caused by larger forces in the economy such as agricultural crops and production cycles. (And indeed, recent research confirms that the average time between stock-market lows in the past 100 years, as measured by the Dow Jones Industrial Average, has been about four years.)

In short, demand in the real economy was anticipated in stock prices, causing them to rise or fall. "The stock market is in the nature of a barometer which reflects the rise and fall of general conditions," Dow wrote in 1899. The fallout from Dow's work—and from his creation of the Dow Jones Industrial Average in 1896 in order to precisely measure the movement of the market—spawned the development of technical analysis.

Technical analysts see movement in the market as a series of patterns, cycles, or waves. Waves can variously be smaller, shorter, bigger, or longer. And, like the ocean, there are also tidal waves when these small waves merge into much larger ones. In the stock market, the emotions of human beings create these waves of buying and selling.

The graphical form of expressing the fulfilment of these human emotions—greed and fear predominantly—is what technical analysis is all about. Whether they be Dow followers or not, these analysts chart the cyclical patterns of the market, using intricate methods of tracking stock-price movements. Then they read these charts to predict the future, based on the past. They have their own language to describe it: not only waves and cycles, but also grand cycles, head-and-shoulders patterns, double dips and double tops, moving averages, momentum. These are the Prechters, the Richard Russells, the Ian McAvitys.

The opposing camp in divining market behaviour is the fundamental-analysis contingent, who base their analysis on economic statistics and corporations' financial results and the prospects for a company in its market. They believe the stock market is a rational mechanism understandable in the context of intrinsic values. Where once these analysts closely followed freight-car loading or the money supply, today the most spellbinding statistics are the consumer price index and labour-force growth.

The fundamentalist camp has as one of its seminal moments in history the publication of the book *Security Analysis* by Benjamin Graham and David Dodd, which set out the principles for "value investing," emphasizing that the underlying values of a stock should be reflected in the price, and that return was the single most important element to a stock buyer. That was the basis of the theory that the greater the risk, the greater the reward.

Fundamental analysis is not very helpful in assessing new ventures or in major exploration plays or when new management is brought into a company. An example is Barrick Resources (now called Barrick Gold Corp.), which originally came to market at $1 in 1983. For three or four years, nobody wanted to touch it. The stock had to go over $10 before anyone would consider buying it. What was needed was faith in the management of the company, namely, its chairman Peter Munk, in order to buy the stock or the story that went with it. There was no support from the fundamental analysts. Today, there is hardly a day that passes when a new research report isn't issued on the company. But the stock hardly moves.

Microsoft is another good example. In its formative years, there were no analysts who could have predicted that the company's market capitalization could exceed $1 billion. Nor were analysts very helpful in picking up the fundamental mistake of IBM in sticking with large-frame computers and ignoring personal computers. That decision caused IBM to decline from $170 to below $50. Once IBM installed new management and rectified that crucial error, its stock became the darling of the Street.

Of course, everybody believes the grass is greener elsewhere, and in today's market you have technical analysts who want to become traders and you have really good traders who want to become fundamentalist thinkers; and nobody admits that they lack the discipline or the mental capability to be both. This is why you will find that the people who are very good at calling the market make their money by doing just that. Robert Prechter, Jr., and Martin Zweig are not going to play the market: they get rich selling market advice—selling subscriptions at $250–$1,000 a year.

As a result, people who are most objective and draw on technical analysis of markets make the worst traders. No one would call my friend Ian McAvity a rich man, but he is one of the best technical analysts around. I have absolutely no abilities as a technical analyst; I am a trader and, as my partner Hal Jones likes to point out, I can make $400,000 in one morning and not hold a position for more than twenty-eight minutes.

They are completely different skills, requiring completely different temperaments. That's why the best analysts are never rich, and why traders who know all the tricks in the book are not able to do technical analysis or to predict the market. They need the feel of the marketplace, the feel of the numbers and the movements, and then they play accordingly. The perfect combination is to have three skills: an understanding of the technical work, an understanding of the fundamental research, and an ability to trade. Not many people have all that.

To assess the stock market correctly, it is necessary to take into account both technical and fundamental analysis. Most people are familiar with fundamentals. They hear about job-market increases or inflation or manufacturers' inventories on a daily basis. But most economic factors cannot, in themselves, "turn" the market—at least, not until they have become extreme in nature. However, economics do influence the thinking of business, which in turn can influence the market.

Because I am a trader first and foremost, I believe that emotion overwhelmingly rules the stock market. I also believe that the analysis of market psychology is more valuable to the investor than fundamental analysis. How markets behave—how people in those markets behave—is the final determinant of where stock prices will go.

How do the market phantoms of fear and greed affect mass-investor psychology and how does mass psychology affect the movement of stock prices?

The key to understanding stock markets—and especially bear markets—is to understand investor psychology, in my opinion. Ask yourself what stock prices are. They are merely people's opinions on the value of shares in a company—valuations. The same, of course, is true in any other market: art, real estate, horseflesh. The market itself is made up of many people's opinions on many things.

To grasp the character and direction of the market you must understand people and their motivations. To make money you must *generally* act contrary to the majority opinion. Mass thinking tends to be extremist thinking—this is seen all the time in politics. When people declare that the market simply *can't* go down, that's when you know that it can.

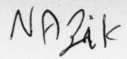

I say generally because the old market adage "don't fight the trend" remains paramount. There is a difference between fighting an established market trend and being a contrarian, someone who stays ahead of the crowd and shifts when the trend shifts. (That's why selling stockholdings before the top, or, if you must, just after the bear moves in, is a much wiser strategy than holding and hoping. By cashing out and buying back in later, you are moving with the market trend.)

Rather, being contrarian involves reading the crowd. When opinion leaders said in May 1962, "This is not another 1929" and "There is no panic," and some said, "This is a time to buy," you can bet on the opposite. Sure enough, the early 1962 market decline lost many times more dollars, adjusted for inflation, than did the Crash of 1929.

Another example: at the end of 1959, economists came out with fearless forecasts of "The Golden Sixties," which promised robust economic health and a booming stock market. Eventually they were right. But almost as soon as they were published, a bear market ensued. The market hit bottom in October 1960 and, by that point, the consensus was one of doom and gloom. In early 1962, most analysts forecasted that the market would be anywhere from very good to mildly good. They didn't call for a crash, but that's precisely what happened.

I am convinced that people get into trouble in the stock market because their emotions rule their thinking. It is in our nature to be happy to be one of the crowd, to be part of a wave of optimism or pessimism.

A lot of work has been done over the years on the nature of crowd behaviour and the extremes it produces. There is, as a nineteenth-century example, Gustave LeBon's *The Crowd*. And the classic, even with its shortcomings, is Charles Mackay's *Extraordinary Popular Delusions and the Madness of Crowds*, which detailed the great investment manias of history such as that for Dutch tulips and for the South Seas Bubble.

The crowd is usually wrong. By that I mean, when there is no division of opinion, popular consensus is almost always mistaken. My own rule is that if the vast majority, say, 80 per cent or more, believes something, I make a contrary bet. The stock market, like life in general, is in a constant state of flux. An opinion that is sound today is out of date a year from now—or a month from now. The circumstances that caused people to think in a particular way have changed. By the time everyone has come around to a line of thinking, it is no longer valid. And, quite often, its opposite is valid.

There was a period of time in the stock market when "odd-lot" stock purchases were a terrific monitor of the market thinking of the unsophisticated individual investor. A "lot" is 100 shares. "Odd lots" are small parcels of stock of fewer than 100 shares—the kind bought by individuals investing smaller amounts of money. Today, those investors tend to buy mutual funds when they play the market. In the 1960s, there was a much higher volume of odd-lot buying than today and, as an indicator of crowd psychology, odd-lotters were very useful. Just to illustrate how profoundly wrong the mass thinker is, consider this: For some years at the end of the 1950s, odd-lot short selling consistently stayed below 3,000 lots per day on the New York Stock Exchange. But, in October 1960, when the Dow languished at about 567 points, the odd-lot shorts crept up to 10,000 a day. At that point they were completely and utterly wrong about where the market was headed. The Dow moved up sharply by more than 100 points by February.

In the 1970s, when stock prices were depressed, there were continuous redemptions by individuals holding mutual funds. The number of investment clubs fell dramatically. Just before the Crash of '87, cash inflows to mutual funds from the public took a sharp upturn. In 1988, just ahead of the recovery, there was a stampede out. In Japan, when the Nikkei reached bottom at 14194 points in August 1992, very few investors had the courage to buy. Once again, just before the Japanese market began its recovery, small investors were still selling. At the peak of a market, people are afraid to miss out on further price increases and, at the bottom, they fear it will go lower. In a bear market there comes a point where the investor becomes desperate and will sell at any price. He or she cannot tolerate the pain of those paper losses anymore. Near every market bottom, market "experts" will surface with dire predictions of how much lower prices will go. Having already endured more than they ever dreamed possible, the last of the weak holders react to such prognostications by tossing in the towel at the least propitious point possible.

Emotions are the enemy of the stock market investor. Most people think of themselves as calm, clear thinkers who do reasonable things. But, in truth, most of us are unable to analyse situations in the market with objectivity because we are governed by how we feel, not by what we know. Being emotional, we lose control and act impulsively and irrationally. That is why investors ignore the warning signs that the market is about to take a major turn. We hear and see what we want to.

Fear is the strongest emotion in the market—and certainly the strongest in a bear market—and it does the worst damage. It was responsible for investors crazy with fear that they will miss out on "the next Bre-X," throwing their money at fleecing operations like Timbuktu Minerals, the gold exploration outfit caught with their assays salted. It is responsible for the classic mistake of selling at the bottom of a market and buying higher when confidence returns, only to sell again at a loss.

How does it work? In the market, fear grapples with hope every day. At certain times there's far more of one than the other. In bull markets, optimism and ebullience most often reign supreme. Eventually a sense of infallibility seizes the investor: stock prices have risen in the past, so they will do so in the future. That's when you see stock buyers snapping up equities almost indiscriminately. In the stock market the emotions of the human beings in it create waves of buying and selling. Historian Robert Sobel put it this way in *Panic on Wall Street*: "Bull markets feed on an illusion of endless expansion, unstoppable by any human agency; panics are marked by fears of bottomless decline, which none seem able to arrest."

"Talk" is an important contributor to the formation of a mass psychology in the market. At every market top, people talk about why such prices are logical and legitimate. It happened in the late 1960s, and it is happening in the late 1990s. At the bottom of a market, the talk is of the "end of equities" and why stock investments will never come back. This happened in the 1970s. Today, the incredible appetite for equity mutual funds is based on optimism. People believe stock prices are headed further up, and they are afraid to miss out. The market economy rules the world, opportunities for many companies seem boundless, and there is little competition for the investment dollar from interest-bearing instruments or real estate. Academics and market gurus feed this optimism further by promoting stocks as a better long-run investment than bonds or cash. Optimism overtakes reality. Buyers are seized with a mania; they think prices will keep going up. But, when you think about it, when prices go up, demand diminishes and, when prices fall, demand usually rises. During Boxing Day sales, when prices are slashed, people storm the stores for the bargains. However, in the equities market, people rush in to buy more stock as prices go higher, and they rush to sell as prices go lower. Why? Because market manias are not based on need, but on fear and greed.

There are a variety of theories on why stock prices move up and down. Standard academic theories hold that the sources of market and stock movements can be traced back in a logical manner to fundamental shocks affecting the economy, changes in technology, consumer preferences, demographics, natural resources, and monetary policy or government regulation. Another view is that, over the long term, investors move money in and out of investments in response to changing fundamentals. When stocks become too expensive, investors reduce the demand for them by shifting out of the market, thereby affecting their price.

Historically, the view has been that the market psychology explains market behaviour. These are the shifts in confidence, mood, or enthusiasm for speculation. The evidence that changes in public opinion about the stock market—investor psychology—precipitate stock movements is largely anecdotal, but nonetheless compelling. When the furore erupted over whether Bre-X had actually found any gold in Busang, not only that stock cratered, but so did pretty well every other junior exploration stock—regardless of the risk involved. In a matter of days, sentiment in the market for mining stocks went from overwhelmingly positive to strongly negative.

Markets move when the public, acting on emotion, changes its mind about what lies in the future. Bear and bull markets take time to form as people join the bandwagon. At the end of a long bear market, there are very few believers at first. But gradually more cross over, and finally the overwhelming majority are won over as the belief that the price will rise becomes the prevailing opinion. That is the point at which a market is most likely to decisively change direction—not when there is tremendous conflicting opinion.

For years academics and stock market professionals have debated the validity of the efficient-markets hypothesis, which holds that analysing stocks on a fundamental basis is a waste of time because all available information on stocks is reflected in current prices. Dartboard picks frequently win stock-picking contests held by financial newspapers, seeming to prove this theory. But there are also some legendary investors such as Warren Buffett and George Soros who consistently beat the indexes, and that would seem to disprove the theory. Soros is a daring trader who once had the guts to short the British pound, risking hundreds of millions of dollars of his own and his managed fund's money. Buffett, who calls himself a value investor, believes in buying a stock in order to own the underlying business—not to own the stock.

The idea that stock prices everywhere and at all times reflect the best available knowledge of all relevant information was probably first raised in the 1920s. But the Crash of '29 put an end to it until the theory enjoyed a revived popularity in the 1960s with Burton Malkiel's book *A Random Walk on Wall Street*. The presumption in academic finance, of which Malkiel is a believer, is that statistical evidence overwhelmingly supports the "efficient markets" theory.

As an example, Robert Barsky of the University of Michigan and J. Bradford de Long of Harvard University, writing in the *Journal of Economic History* in 1990, argued that the huge swings in the stock market this century which registered "such a large re-evaluation of the worth of America's companies would also have made any investor uncertain of the possibly changing long-run dividend growth rate who estimated it by extrapolating the recent past. Such revaluations were also made by investment analysts who were prominent in their day, whose acumen we respect, and who concentrated on fundamental values." The major bull and bear swings "arose not because investors' susceptibility to fads and fashions made the market excessively volatile, but because the future always appeared uncertain, and stock prices are extremely sensitive to expectations of what future [economic] growth will be."

Interestingly, however, Barsky and de Long do allow for faulty investor judgement, in that the stock market and its players continually overreact to economic signals. In other words, things are never as good as they seem in a boom, nor as bad as they seem in a depression. And the proof is that this century's major market movements have been reversed more often than not.

How else do we explain the tremendous volatility of stock prices relative to their underlying fundamental value (considered the present value of future dividends)—especially in major bull and bear markets? Why do ten-year real percentage changes in the S&P index demonstrate a volatility that is ten times that of the ten-year percentage changes in the GNP if the index's basket of stocks reflects the overall U.S. economy?

The popular belief, as espoused by a number of important American economists and stock market analysts, is the "animal spirits" of investors. John Kenneth Galbraith, Robert Sobel, and Robert Shiller, among others, have written extensively on this. Galbraith argues that the stock market boom of the 1920s was entirely due to the flood of money from uninformed new investors who were following the "fads and fashions" of the time.

Writing on the postwar bull market that began in 1949, Sobel argued that, if stock prices of the day had truly been solely a reflection of "realities," then the bull would have started years earlier. Rather, he posited, it was only after investors had wiped the memory of the 1929 crash and the subsequent bear from their minds that optimism could take hold—and the great bull market of the 1950s begin. Generally, it takes a new generation of investors to make a bull market.

Robert Shiller, whose important book *Market Volatility* tackled the question of what makes markets move, argued that all the evidence—or most of it—supports the view that "fad and fashions" are the "true source of the bulk of price movements that characterize the aggregate stock market." He argued that too little attention and research have been focused on market psychology as the leading factor in market swings and that the work that has been done on crowd behaviour supports the idea that speculative markets are influenced by capricious changes in investor sentiments. "Various speculative assets are at times overvalued because they are fashionable and have attracted undue attention while other speculative assets are subject to adverse prejudice or are just ignored and hence underpriced."

According to Shiller, people are attracted to a market by observed price increases. Observing these price increases means observing other people becoming rich, and this interests and excites potential investors. Price increases themselves thus cause greater subsequent price increases until the price reaches some barrier. Then the bubble bursts and prices drop precipitously because there are not further price increases to sustain the high demand. A bubble, in Shiller's terms, becomes a bubble and not a fad when price is the "contagion."

In studies on gambling behaviour, the historical stock market anecdotal evidence demonstrates that excessive enthusiasm for certain financial assets leads to exclusion of other investments even if there are excellent reasons for including them in a portfolio. Psychological studies on salience and human judgement show that popular attention to certain speculative assets is capricious in that people don't base their decisions on all the facts and allow themselves to be distracted by attention-grabbing events. Most important, research on group polarization of attitudes supports the intuitive claim that groups of individuals tend to act together and reach the same decisions around the same time. Furthermore, individuals who were less cautious than the population average tended to become even less cautious in groups. One survey on group polarization concluded that "seldom in the history of social psychology has a nonobvious phenomenon been so firmly grounded in data from across a variety of cultures and dependent measures." To me, this explains much about a financial bubble.

A major bear market isn't one-dimensional any more than a major bull is. Consider the bull market of the past fourteen years: despite its tremendous overall rise, it has been marked by significant lows. A long-term bear market, like the bull that precedes it, is a roller-coaster ride—only in the opposite direction. Often, although not always, a bear begins with a heart-stopping crash over a few days. Panic seizes everybody in the market as they try desperately to get out and then discover that doing so is not that easy. I remember in October 1989 when a major takeover deal involving United Airlines failed to materialize. It so rocked the confidence of investors in the market that stocks went into a tailspin for two days. For two days, you literally could not find anyone to sell your stocks to: there were no bids in the market.

A major bear traces a long, slow decline, but within it are very rapid, steep upward moves. Each of these successive waves down and up sinks the market lower. The up ticks don't last very long either, but they do give the investor the feeling that the gloom is lifting and the bear is on his way out—that is, until the next wave down begins.

Following the Great Crash of 1929, there were a number of rallies in 1930 before the terrible bear truly set in. Despite the horrible financial devastation of the year before, there was still hope in the market—there were many people on Wall Street who were convinced that another bull market was not only possible, but already under way. "Even in 1929, after one of the most dramatic selloffs in market history, most analysts found it difficult to believe that they were in the initial stage of a major bear market," writes Robert Sobel. Indeed, in the period 1929–34, there were people who continued to believe that the free-fall in stock prices couldn't be happening and that an optimistic view would overcome market forces.

The effect of a bear is to wring out the excesses of a speculative period, and that often takes a great deal of time and agony. Those secondary reactions serve the purpose. Those sharp up ticks in an otherwise southbound market seem to indicate that prices are headed back up. They offer investors a reason for optimism in spite of abundant evidence to the contrary. They give investors just enough hope to keep going.

That hope, of course, creates a market for stocks. So who buys in a bear market? Some are those who've changed their minds about the direction of the market and were waiting to buy cheaper. They help support the dips. After a collapse in prices, the market becomes temporarily oversold. But there remains a pool of buyers who believe that any price is a bargain just because it is substantially lower—they are the ones making their decisions based on the past. As well, there are those who went short at higher levels who now decide to take some profits. It is this combination that creates significant rallies in bear markets.

When the bear resumes its course, investors are then stripped not only of hope, but also of the value of their investments. Every "leg" or phase of a bear market is interrupted by one of these rallies. They are useful to those who want to salvage something from their stockholdings if they did not bail out of the market earlier. They also present an opportunity for shorting. These up ticks continue to occur as long as there are enough people available to change their minds about the market.

As the process of changing opinion makes the market move, once everyone's mind is made up, the movement in one directions stops and the market tends to reverse direction just as everybody climbs on board.

People tend to live with yesterday's problem (rather than today's) when making investment decisions. An example is the "Sideways Bear" of 1946–49, when bonds paid 2.5 per cent and the inflation rate was above that. Investors kept those bonds because they feared a 1930s-type of situation, and as a result they effectively lost 90 per cent of their money. At the time, the Bank of Montreal was the leading bank in Canada. Its executives were busy preparing the bank for what they believed was the coming depression while, at the Royal Bank, executives were preparing for a major expansion. They were the ones who were right, because they avoided judging the future based on their experiences of the past.

Pessimism, doubt, and uncertainty rule in a bear. The pervading sense that things can go very wrong because they already have is a response to what has happened in the past rather than a reaction to what could happen in the future. Because of that, we are blind to the signs of a turning point and have no appetite for equities, no matter how cheaply they are priced and how logical the argument for buying them—or, conversely, how outrageously high they are priced, and how illogical the argument for them going up still further in price.

The real difference between bull markets and bear markets is their pace. Bear markets are slow. They are not generally characterized by the big dramatic breaks, such as the crash of 1987. Rather, there is a slow, grinding, demoralizing erosion of values. The bear moves through groups of stocks, taking its toll. One day or week or month, it is retail stocks; the next, bank stocks, followed by oil-and gas- or commodity-based issues. The bear moves patiently through each sector, one by one. The last to fall are the top-quality stocks, once known as "Nifty Fifty" stocks, which have the largest weighting in the stock indexes. That is when you can measure the damage on the Dow. And that is why one specific group of stocks can get hammered—such as the high-tech stocks during the summer of 1996—while the widely quoted indexes are still hitting highs.

No two bull or bear markets are exactly alike, although they do all have some similarities. Bear markets have been as short as two months and as long as five years. Generally, the blue-chips don't fall as far as the vast majority of stocks—although that wasn't the case in 1973. Not all bears begin with a heart-stopping crash over the course of a few days. The bear of 1969 began with a barely noticeable slide. Some are one-crash wonders, like 1987. But the bear of 1929 featured six successive market crashes over thirty-four months. And then there was the sideways bear of 1946–49, when the market literally went nowhere (trading in a very narrow range between 163 and 193 points) for three years following a 25 per cent decline.

Unfortunately, there is never a convenient warning signal saying a bear market is about to begin. However, there are always conditions in the market that give the wise, experienced investor an uncomfortable feeling that a big break is in the offing. Remember the old saying: "The market always does what it should do, but not when it should."

The most serious declines in stock market history have started with what looked like a series of meaningless light volume declines. They seemed to be simply temporary setbacks. When prices start to fall, pundits talk about profit-taking. Most people don't sell at this stage; rather, they think of it as a buying opportunity. "Buy the dips!"

Only after the decline has truly set in do people begin to panic and dump stocks. Some will start to short to recoup their losses. (To short a stock, an investor contracts to sell it at some future date without actually owning it: the bet is that he or she will be able to buy it for less than he or she is committed to sell it at.) Most people make a decision to liquidate when prices have dropped a great deal and it is harder to sell. However, one important lesson for a bear market is that the loss of a top price, or even an actual loss from cost, is better than the risk of holding onto something as it plummets in value. "The investor who panics first, panics best" is cautionary wisdom.

Recall my simple description of the marketplace and how tops and bottoms occur: Every transaction has a buyer on one side and a seller on the other. Every price change—up or down—is implicitly driven by one or the other "reaching" to make the trade occur. The buyer reaches up to motivate a transaction, or the seller reaches down to hit a bid. High and low points in the market can be characterized as the point at which the last buyer bought or the last seller sold.

Now consider the real world of the market. Portfolio managers, who after all are custodians of other people's money, cannot be investors in the tradition of Warren Buffett and Max Tanenbaum. Those two men believed in investing for the very long term and liked price weaknesses because they could accumulate all the more stock in their favourite companies. (Max was influential in my early career when he showed great faith in handing me $250,000 to give me a start as a professional money manager in 1974, at the bottom of the bear market; through Max I learned to respect value investing, but I also became aware of the risks.)

Fund managers, on the other hand, must keep in mind that fund investors can call their money any time, so the fund must maintain significant cash positions. In a panic-stricken and falling market, redemptions skyrocket, and those cash reserves can be used up very quickly. When they are, portfolio managers are forced to dump stock on the market in order to raise more cash. That's when the real bear market gets going: when this additional stock is put on the market without additional buying power being present.

The search for buyers for these extra stocks in a declining market depresses prices further and further. When finally even individual investors—the least savvy group in the market—have sold out their positions and taken their money out of harm's way, then there are no more sellers and no more buyers. That is when the market turns. The scramble then is to find the best values at rock-bottom prices.

But along the way to that turning point, there are a number of phases and many tricks from the bear, including the false hope of a quick recovery.

Here is how *Forbes*, on July 15, 1962, painted the bear-market scenario: "Then suddenly there comes a turn in the market and stocks are going up as fast as they have come down. The hapless speculator will wait a few days to see whether this rally is genuine and then he will cover his shorts, buy stocks on margin (to make up for his losses) and by the time the rally falters and the bear market resumes its decline, he will be fully invested once again and ready to be slaughtered in the same way."

History shows that bear markets tend to last a third to one-half as long as their preceding bull market. Thus, two months after the 1929 crash, a supposed bull-market signal seemed improbable—although many people believed it anyway. The lessons of a major bear market obviously are not lost on those who felt it first-hand. That is why it often takes a long period of time for another bull market to get rolling. The collective memory of the financial devastation of a market crash makes investors cautious and wary. But eventually, as with the bull market that got rolling in the postwar years, the sting of the bear's claws fades from memory and people are once again willing to jump on the bandwagon. For most people, this is long after the bull has begun, and long after the big exponential profits have been made.

Those investors courageous enough to buy stocks at the turn of a market are not those who were in the previous market. One example is the pattern of market crises of the nineteenth century in the United States. European investors in the American stock market were greatly harmed by the panics of 1792, 1837, 1857, 1873, 1893, and 1907 and, as a result, avoided the American market as it recovered from each of those sell-offs. Meanwhile, "native speculators and investors made fortunes by purchasing securities at depressed prices. Then, when the next boom was at a mature stage, these securities would be resold to for-eigners"—who had finally recovered their nerve—"who once again would lose their fortunes in the crash which shortly came thereafter." Robert Sobel makes the argument that this was so because the Americans knew their own market so much better than even the most sophisticated European investor.

In today's market, the role of the nineteenth-century foreign investors is played by the unsophisticated individual who generally waits at least two years into a bull before jumping in. Between 1984 and the present, the S&P 500 index has risen 800 per cent. However, the investing public hasn't made that much for two reasons: funds don't perform as well as the indexes normally, and fundholders must pay fees to managers. Those are the same investors who waited to buy into the Mexico stock market until just before its crash at the end of 1994, and the same ones who were so enthusiastic for technology stocks in 1996—after they had their big run-up the year before.

I believe that the investors who really know the market today—which means those who have the best access to information about it—are the institutions and professional investors. The Internet has changed things somewhat in allowing rumours to sweep through a market faster and to move those rumours from the Street to the kitchen-table investor. For that reason, the small investor has the illu-sion that he or she is on more of an equal footing with the pros. But that is not the case. The pros always get the news first; they also watch the Internet and they trade in, not just seconds, but fractions of seconds. They are the ones who make the big money at the start of the bull mar-ket, and they are the ones who take their profits by selling stocks to individuals who jump in late in the game, the ones who have shovelled their billions of savings into mutual funds in the last few years.

CHAPTER FIVE

The Virtuous and the Vicious: The Lessons of History

"The less a man knows about the past and the present, the more insecure must be his judgment of the future."

—SIGMUND FREUD

Every market in the history of investment has had its times of speculative euphoria. Every generation witnesses a crash, its moments of panic, and its periods of contraction and decline. Buyers and sellers in the eternal dance of commerce are always looking for each other and finding either too few or too many. That is what sets prices for houses, tulip bulbs, stocks, or gold bullion. But two other partners must be on the dance floor for the truly breathtaking manias and panics to play out: greed and fear.

There have been many famous manias and panics throughout commercial history: the well-known Dutch tulip-bulb mania of 1634–37, where over a period of thirty-six months prices of tulip bulbs rose 5900 per cent, then declined over ten months by 93 per cent; the South Seas shares mania in Britain in 1719–20, where over eight months investors pushed shares up 1000 per cent and then saw them plummet 84 per cent over six months; the American stock market of the 1920s, where equities rose in price 354 per cent, then fell an average of 87 per cent; the silver mania of 1979–82, where its value increased 710 per cent over twelve months, and then dropped 88 per cent over twenty-four months. The bubble in the Hong Kong stock market during the period 1970–74 was one of the most amazing in history. The share index there went from 345 to 1711, and back to 401 a year later—overall, it was up 1200 per cent over twenty-eight months before collapsing 92 per cent over twenty months. These manias all featured frenzied crowd participation and massive rises in prices, followed by sheer panic as those prices dropped through the floor.

Market historian Robert Sobel, in his book *Panic on Wall Street*, listed a few of the conclusions market watchers of the past had come to learn about "panics":

- Most panics occur during periods of optimism. In 1791, speculators saw great possibilities for investment; the West beckoned in 1836; railroads were magic in 1857, and again in 1873, 1901, and 1907. Everything seemed headed upward in 1929, and new industries provided glamour for 1962.
- Most panics were made possible, though were not necessarily caused, by weakness in the financial structure.
- Most panics occur as "moments of truth" after periods of self-deception.

The U.S. stock market has experienced five major bull and bear phases thus far in the twentieth century. The two worst bear markets were both preceded by two years of speculative mania. The Great Crash of 1929, which really continued to 1932, had a number of causes, but prime among them was dubious credit, which supported stock prices, iffy trading practices on Wall Street, and a downturn in industrial production.

The 1969–74 bear was triggered by the spectre of inflation. The bull market that preceded it and the bear itself hold great lessons for investors of today. The tremendous, sudden meltdown of 1929 did not occur as the market went into a bear phase in 1969. It was not as swift, dramatic, and intense, although the decline that took place over the course of 1973 saw stock prices plummet by 50 per cent.

Spectacular crashes often herald the end of a major bull market, but there are no similar signals to mark the beginning of a bull. There was none in 1924, when the great move up was about to start, and no indication in 1949 that a postwar bull was under way. "Market crashes are usually visible only in retrospect. If prices tumble, but then recover, and go on to new highs, the dip is termed a 'correction'; only when they continue to fall does it become a crash. Similarly, the switch from a bull to bear market can best be studied ex post facto," Sobel has written.

A major bull market cannot be started or sustained without investors, that is, holders and buyers of blue-chips. They provide the foundation for all major advances. At the start of the great bull market of the 1950s and 1960s, the New York Stock Exchange was a playground for traders. Ordinary people, still mindful of the crash of 1929 and its aftermath, were far away from the stock market.

The nature of traders is that they move in and out of the market quickly; they are skittish; they are quick to take their profits. Their activities cause prices to decline after they make a small advance. Investors arriving on the scene change the tenor of the marketplace. Their purchases are regular, they retain stocks during advances, they even add new shares to their portfolios on declines. Trading volume becomes steadier and gives the market continuity. Attracted by higher prices, speculators arrive, adding glamour to the scene—and this is a major factor in any major bull market. But without the small investor it doesn't happen.

It is usually difficult to convince small investors that the purchase and holding of stocks is sensible and prudent. But once these investors have had a taste of big returns, they are reluctant to abandon their hopes of capital gains. "Small investors are the first to arrive at the feast and the last to leave. Very often they manage to get in on the ground floor of bull markets but they remain too long and may be forced to leap from the roof in the end," wrote Sobel.

Like the mutual fund buyers of today, individuals in the 1950s were attracted to the stock market because blue-chips were paying three or four times as much as savings accounts. Soon enough they were able to make the leap from dividends to capital gains—from "safe" investments to risk. All bull markets begin with an appreciation of economic fundamentals, but they don't truly get going until investors start looking to the future and harbour dreams of capital gains. This happened in the 1920s and in the 1950s–60s, and it is happening today.

The Famous Bubbles

The first major modern stock market was established in Amsterdam in the seventeenth century and was followed by one in London in 1688. According to *The Wall Street Journal*, Joseph de la Bega published a book on how stock markets functioned based on the Amsterdam exchange. Its title was *Confusion of Confusions*.

The three great speculative orgies of the seventeenth and early eighteenth centuries are all well documented in numerous works. These stories of financial bubbles and their ensuing panics and others that followed later are now part of popular history: Tulipomania, the South Sea Islands bubble, John Law's Mississippi scheme, the stock market of the 1920s, the Florida land-price bubble of the 1920s, the Canadian stock boom of the early 1950s (during which uranium mines and Western oil fields were discovered and promoted daily, although aside from a few success stories like Denison Mines and TransCanada PipeLines, very few of them ever produced anything, and most were simply stock promotions), the "growth stock" craze of the 1960s. Common to all of them is an excessive enthusiasm for speculative assets based on unsound judgement.

The most famous cautionary tale is probably the mania for tulip bulbs during 1635–36 in Holland, when single bulbs sold for as much as $50,000 in today's dollars. In Charles Mackay's nineteenth-century classic, *Popular Delusions and the Madness of Crowds* (anybody who believes that these times in the stock market are different should read this book: every financial instrument known today was around then), he wrote, "In 1634, the rage among the Dutch to possess them [tulips] was so great that the ordinary industry of the country was neglected and the population, even to its lowest dregs, embarked in the tulip trade. As the mania increased, prices augmented until, in 1635, many persons were known to invest a fortune of 100,000 Florins in the purchase of 40 roots ... Houses and land were offered for sale at ruinously low prices, or assigned in payment of bargains made at the tulip market." When the bubble burst, there was widespread ruin among the population.

"Every one imagined that the passion for tulips would last forever, and that the wealthy from every part of the world would send to Holland and pay whatever prices were asked for them ... Nobels, citizens, farmers, mechanics, seamen, footmen, maid-servants, even chimney-sweeps and old clotheswomen, dabbled in tulips."

The credulity of investors helped create the South Sea bubble, a financial crisis that ruined thousands in Britain in 1719–20. Speculation largely centred on the South Sea Company, which had a monopoly on trade with South America, shares of which soared by 680 per cent in seven months before crashing. But other smaller bubble companies also drew feverish speculation. Some were legitimate, such as the Sun Insurance Company, but many were outright frauds. One company's prospectus declared it was created "for carrying on an undertaking of great advantage, but nobody is to know what it is."

The mania to buy a piece of John Law's Mississippi Company, before it collapsed on the Paris exchange in 1720, was such that women offered their bodies for the right to buy shares. John Law, a Scottish-born rapscallion with a track record for dubious financial engineering, established the company to explore for gold in the presumed rich territory of Louisiana, in North America. Galbraith tells it in amusing style in his 1990 book, *A Short History of Financial Euphoria*: "There was no evidence of the gold, but this, as ever in such episodes, was no time for doubters or doubting. Shares of the company were offered to the public and the response was sensational." The proceeds from the share issues were circulated through Law's chartered bank, the Banque Royale, and to the government to help pay the enormous national debt. "The notes that went out to pay the debt came back to buy more stock. More stock was then issued to satisfy more of the intense demand, the latter having the effect of lifting both the old and the new issues to ever more extravagant heights." It was a classic virtuous circle.

The end came, as Galbraith describes it, when a French nobleman, annoyed because he couldn't buy some Mississippi Company stock, sent his notes in to Banque Royale for redemption in gold. This caused others to think gold might be better than notes, and a run on the bank ensued. On one day, fifteen people were killed in the crush in front of the bank. When the bank declared the notes no longer convertible into gold, not only Mississippi Company shares but other assets collapsed in value. "Citizens who a week before had been millionaires—an indispensable term that was given to us by these years—were now impoverished," wrote Galbraith.

By the nineteenth century, the New World was experiencing more than its share of speculative orgies in all manner of things—and its share of collapses and panics. In the early 1830s, skyrocketing prices for cotton and a boom in canal construction led to a frenzy for property and banking shares. In Chicago, a land boom sprang up at that time and, within a few years, land prices rose a hundredfold. But, as with all high-flying markets, it all came to an end in 1837, when a financial crisis developed after Chicago property prices plunged 90 per cent and canal building came almost to a halt. The trigger for the collapse was not unlike what could happen to the present stock market. In 1836, British gold reserves fell by almost 50 per cent because so much wealth was flowing out of Britain to America for purchases of securities there. The Bank of England was twice forced to increase the rediscount rate in order to curb the flow. That led to a monetary panic in Britain and the closure of several banks. Higher interest rates in Britain (the call rate rose to about 15 per cent) cut off demand for American securities almost overnight. (Once again, liquidity is the key factor in manias and collapses.) This came at precisely the time when demand for money in the United States was at its highest. The sudden disappearance of foreign capital had a devastating effect on the American economy, abruptly choking off growth and putting an almost immediate halt to canal and railroad construction.

The Gold Mania

Gold is the oldest and purest form of money on the planet. It is backed by thousands of years of history as a true store of value, and it is the only financial asset that is not at the same time a liability of some other party.

The price of gold was fixed for centuries: Britain fixed it from 1717 to 1914, and the United States took over in 1934 and kept it fixed for another thirty-six years. But in 1970, mounting inflationary pressure in the United States forced Washington to allow gold to find its own price in the marketplace or risk sending the country into deflation.

In this modern world of plastic cards and ATMs, many see gold as some sort of historic relic, unnecessary in these overconfident times. But for anyone like myself, with a keen understanding of the dangers of undisciplined currencies, gold remains the only form of insurance against a devastating loss of purchasing power. My formative years were spent in Hungary, and in 1945–46, while I was in my mid-teens, the country experienced a great classical inflation, during which money lost its value faster than the government could print new currency. Eventually it was counted in the billions and hundreds of billions. The one stable currency was gold; it had the magical power of putting groceries on the table and fuel in the furnace. Ever since that lesson, I do not put all my faith in paper currency. Gold is most useful as a defensive investment. It acts the way accident or fire insurance does—it gives you a sense of security, allows you to sleep soundly at night, but it is not the path to enrichment.

Having said that, gold does attract speculation during inflationary cycles of the economy. Inflation tends to pick up speed in the latter stages of the business cycle—when the economy reaches full expansion. Early in the business cycle, the financial asset categories are favoured. Look at the stock markets (and the funds that played them) in the Pacific Region during the past few years. But as stocks, and particularly hot regional markets, begin to wind down, base metals and precious metals take on their own lustre.

The last gold rush ended with gold reaching $850 in January 1980.

It started its climb nine years before, in 1971, at $35 an ounce. By year-end 1974, the price had peaked at $197.50 in anticipation of the U.S. government finally allowing Americans to own gold privately, but gold fell back to $103.50 when an anticipated enthusiasm for it did not materialize. A few years later, however, gold had a completely irrational rise in price over an incredibly short period of time. It began when the precious metal crossed the $400 level at the end of November 1979. Just seven weeks later, it hit $850 (its all-time high, as it turned out), only to collapse to $624 a week later. It bottomed in March at $474. Later that year, in September, gold rallied to $720, but failed to maintain that price level. It was a classic bear-market rally, pulling in the last few suckers. In early 1982, the price held around the $500 mark, but ultimately gold fell to a bottom of $297 in February 1985. It has been in a long sideways bear market ever since.

That incredible mania of the late 1970s was an aberration. It was based on fear that the dollar would become worthless and that inflation would accelerate. Gold was seen as a safe haven. There was a classic panic to buy.

My friend Peter de Sario was managing a futures brokerage house in the early 1980s, and in January 1980, with gold soaring to over $700 an ounce, he predicted to clients and colleagues that the gold market was headed for a swift and substantial price drop. His audience immediately told him he was completely wrong. On January 21, gold and silver peaked, and de Sario remembers to this day that his office was swamped with calls from clients, some who had never traded a futures contract before, inquiring about buying gold and silver. One aspiring speculator told him that he wanted to buy silver while it was still cheap—even though at that point the price of the metal had increased tenfold in the previous six months, going from $6 an ounce to a high of $50.35.

The reason silver enjoyed such a meteoric rise in price at that time was that two billionaire brothers who had made their fortune in oil, Nelson Bunker and William Herbert Hunt, of Texas, tried to corner the market on silver in 1979. They believed that the world was about to be ruined by hyperinflation. Their plan collapsed, and so did the price of silver, tumbling to $10.80 by March 1980. The Hunt brothers lost roughly $1.3 billion and subsequently were distinguished by being the largest personal bankruptcy in U.S. history. And many small-time speculators, like the chap who called Peter de Sario that day, went down with them.

At the end of the 1970s, almost every investment portfolio still boasted a substantial gold weighting. But from 1981 to 1993, the price was stuck in a narrow trading range of $300 to $500. This sideways movement so depressed the appetite for gold that two of the oldest gold fund groups spent the better part of 1993–94 promoting bond funds and Asian funds rather than their specialty.

The precious metal disappeared from the vast majority of portfolios. Mostly this was because of the poor price performance—between 1987 and 1992 gold lost about 30 per cent!—but, as well, it has surrendered much of its traditional function and is rarely used today as a hedge against inflation. (Although, Mexican families found it useful to own gold a couple of years ago when the peso lost half of its value against the U.S. dollar almost overnight.)

In 1992, gold finally emerged from its long price slump and has edged up to the $450 range in recent years. It has tried and failed to move through the important $500 barrier.

If we accept that gold was priced at $36 an ounce in 1945 and at $450 in 1997, I would argue that gold has more than maintained its value. The deflationary policies created by the continuous sale of gold by the central banks continue even today to depress its price.

The Nikkei Mania

The bull market in Japan in the 1980s was this century's greatest bubble. Driven by highly protected industry, soaring real estate prices, and immense liquidity, Japan had developed into a classic bubble economy by 1990. Golf club memberships were changing hands for $1 million. Stocks were sold door-to-door like magazine subscriptions. Peter Lynch, in his book *Beating the Street*, describes his visit to the Tokyo market: "The advertising slogan 'When E.F. Hutton talks, people listen,' would have been an understatement in Japan. There, the slogan would have been 'When Nomura Securities commands, people obey.' Brokers were entirely trusted and their advice was taken as gospel. The result was a wondrous market of stocks with P/E ratios of 50, 100, 200, which were so out of line with rational levels that bystanders began to theorize that the high Japanese P/E was a cultural trait." A variation on the This Time It's Different theme.

The stock market in Tokyo hit its 38957-point high in 1989, and the equity risk premium in Japan had entered negative territory by the time the speculative binge reached its peak. That meant stocks had become so overpriced that they were likely to substantially underperform bonds. The Japanese bull market had been around for such a long time—since 1962—that stockholders had never known a time when equities didn't go up in price. They literally didn't know things could change.

The Bank of Japan made a decision to take some of the air out of the massive speculative bubble that had developed by raising interest rates. The effect was immediate and brutal. In March 1990, Japanese stocks nosedived by almost 25 per cent, stunning market participants. Volume dropped from 3 billion shares a day to 200 million. That meant nobody got out. They simply marked down the prices. It's an old story, but when liquidity disappears, it is a tremendously ruthless scene.

The débâcle in Tokyo was similar to the bust in real estate in the late 1980s in North America. When one house on the block is for sale for $700,000, that sets the price for all. But when there are two houses for sale, the price changes tremendously. All of a sudden there isn't a matching player on the other side of the sell ticket. The price has to be marked down until a buyer is found. Plenty of people get caught flatfooted. That is how large wealth transfers have taken place over time. In most speculative bubbles, you find at least a 50 per cent drop from the peak. And that is an extremely significant drop, requiring a 100 per cent gain to recoup.

Contributing greatly to the Japanese stock bubble was the practice of Zaiteku, the aggressive investing of Japanese companies, both large and small, in the stocks of other Japanese companies. At its peak,

Zaiteku was a major source of profits for Japanese corporations. For example, in fiscal 1987, it contributed 48 per cent of Toyota's profits, 107 per cent of both Nissan's and Sony's profits, 81 per cent of Sharp's, 58 per cent of Mitsubishi's, 61 per cent of Matsushita's, and 46 per cent of Sumitomo Bank's. By hugely inflating profits, Zaiteku also hugely inflated stock prices. It was a classic virtuous circle: Rising prices meant prices would rise.

The Nikkei index fell 63 per cent over thirty-two months, finally hitting bottom near the 14000 mark. With a few rallies since, the person who bought at the top in 1989 is still down 35 per cent. In fact, in mid-1995 the Nikkei again fell into the 14000 range, as it remained mired in a vicious bear market. Investors who bought in 1989 now need a 360 per cent gain by 1999 to earn a ten-year 10 per cent average return. That is unlikely to happen.

Two bear markets in stocks in North America merit examination today. The Crash of '29 was an event of major historical importance, heralding as it did the Depression of the 1930s. The bear of 1973–74 is well within the scope of many people's personal experience. Although 1929 has received all the publicity—mainly because of the all-encompassing economic and social fallout—as the most devastating financial disaster of all time, that is not entirely accurate. There are those who argue that, for example, 1974 was as bad. Certainly, the economy was very weak for the rest of the decade and into the recession of the early 1980s. Interest rates were high, soaring above 20 per cent for a time. The energy crisis—when the price of oil escalated to $40 a barrel—crippled industry. When the U.S. government imposed odd days and even days at the gas pumps in order to conserve oil supplies, car sales nosedived. General Motors, for one, was close to bankruptcy, losing an average of $50 million a day, month after month.

The overarching tone of the Roaring '20s, if not the details, is known to most people today. This is a measure of the impact the Crash of '29 had on the popular imagination. In the 1920s, almost from the beginning of the bull market in 1922, volume and prices moved up at an astonishing rate. By 1925, the value of all NYSE-listed stocks was about $25 billion. By 1929, that figure was very nearly $100 billion. At the same time, the number of Americans who owned stocks had jumped to 20 million from fewer than 2 million. There were plenty of indications that the bull market was topping long before the crash. The market advanced through the summer of 1929 with a few dips but also a number of rallies, which took the Dow to new highs. However, in September, the market simply failed to continue its success of the summer. At the start of October, the market decline began. Margin calls increased, and talk surfaced of a technical correction. In the third week of October, nervousness about the slide accelerated trading. Volume was heavy. Formerly high-flying stocks showed losses of 5 to 50 points. One fund, considered to be conservative, lost 96 points in a day. The pace of trading continued to quicken, and crowds began gathering outside the stock exchange, sensing something momentous was happening. On Tuesday, October 24, the bottom fell out of the market, with outright dumping of stocks by investors. Liquidations took place all over the nation. By the third week of November, the entire gain of the bull market had been wiped out. But as stunning as that was, the crash was not as important in the end as the long slide in stock values from 1930 to 1934. There were rallies, of course, but it was not until 1954 that the prices at the peak in mid-1929 were seen again.

The 1990s and the 1920s present compelling comparisons. Then, as now, many people, even those with only a small amount to invest, jumped into stocks with the dream of becoming rich. This blind bullishness always downplays the risk involved.

In the 1920s, Americans believed a new era of permanent prosperity had dawned. Perhaps this is best captured by the infamous advice Wall Street speculator John J. Raskob gave to the innocent readers of *Ladies Home Journal* in 1929, when he declared that anyone could become wealthy by putting $15 a month (a substantial sum in those days) into stocks and holding them for the long term. That siren call drew millions of new investors into the market at the top. Today, of course, the allure of prosperity and old-age financial security presented by the mutual funds—all for a few hundred dollars a month—draws millions of neophyte investors, even though the stock market is considered by the pros to be expensive.

Another striking similarity was that mergers, secondary offerings, and stock splits were numerous in the 1920s, as they have been during the mid-1990s. In other words, smart money was selling. Then, as now, the bulls were counting on higher earnings, low inflation, and an expanding economy.

In the 1920s individuals bought on margin—indeed, they were financing much of their lifestyle on credit. By the 1960s, most investors paid cash for their shares. Today, there is a deep suspicion, but little evidence, that many small-time investors are financing their speculation with loans against their homes, or even their credit cards.

The market of the 1920s attracted hordes of the uninitiated, just as the current bull market has.

After declaring everyone ought to be rich, Raskob later refined his financial advice to add that the money should be turned over to a pool for investments and the result would be even better. Investment trusts were an idea from mid-nineteenth-century Britain transplanted to Wall Street, and the ancestor of mutual funds.

At the height of the bull market in 1929, investment trusts had assets, that is, stock and bond holdings, of approximately $4.5 billion. To understand their impact on the market, the capitalization of all U.S. corporations was $183.5 billion. The influence of these investment trusts could cause the market to rise or fall at will—or so ran the popular belief of the day. In August 1929, Goldman Sachs alone floated more than a quarter of a billion dollars' worth of securities as part of its takeover activity. (Raskob, meanwhile, had decided that stock prices had outrun demonstrated values, earning power, and dividend returns, and that a material readjustment was necessary. He didn't make his revised opinion well known, but changed his strategy and sold his holdings. He emerged from the crash a multimillionaire.)

The sudden flood of new investment companies, together with the large fluctuations they produced in 1928 and 1929, created two major, interrelated problems, according to Sobel. One, the investment trusts found it difficult to find investments that would appreciate quickly enough to "make good reading" for potential investors. As well, competition for key stock issues was so intense that they were often bid-up beyond reasonable prices. These are the same problems confronting mutual funds in the 1990s.

In dollar losses, the 1969–74 bear was much more severe than that in 1929–32, although that's not true in percentage terms. The Dow reached a peak in September 1929 of 381 and a low of 41 in July 1932, representing an 89 per cent decline. The S&P index fell by 86 per cent during the same time. (The indexes were more representative of the average stock then.) Professor Robert Klemkosky of the Virginia Polytechnic Institute makes the case that, by the end of 1974, real losses, after adjusting for inflation, far surpassed those suffered in the earlier bear on an absolute-dollar basis and nearly equalled them on a percentage basis.

That said, the economic consequences of the bear of the 1970s were not nearly as severe as those of the "Dirty Thirties." Twenty years elapsed before the losses suffered in 1929–32 were recouped: it was 1950 before the market value of all New York Stock Exchange–listed issues surpassed the level of 1929. It was not until 1954 that the Dow and the S&P indexes surpassed their September 1929 highs. One generation of investors sat out the stock market.

The market's performance from 1950 to 1968 was one of the most favourable in stock market history: The market appreciated 370 per cent in that time, exceeding the total cumulative gain for all of the preceding seventy-nine years from 1871 to 1949. Investors, then as now, could buy just about any type of security and achieve high rates of return. Then, as now, there were few prolonged declines, and those that did occur were brief in duration, lasting no more than ten months.

The reason for the fabulous rise through the 1950s and 1960s was the postwar boom in consumer goods and the unchallenged economic dominance of the United States in the international marketplace. During that time, earnings and dividends skyrocketed, with annual compound growth rates of 8 and 6 per cent, respectively.

The number of individuals owning shares reached 20 million by 1965, from 6.5 million in 1950. By 1970, it was more than 30 million. These people had not experienced the miseries of the Great Crash.

Many other events of the tumultuous 1960s and early 1970s affected stocks: two recessions, the Vietnam War, Watergate, oil shortages, and major corporate bankruptcies. Inflation, however, was by far the biggest single factor in sending equity prices down for six years.

Various stock markets performed differently during the first phase of the bear, which started in December 1968. High-quality blue-chips, as measured by the Dow average and the S&P 500 index, were the least affected. Smaller stocks fell by more than 50 per cent.

Because it takes a 100 per cent increase to recapture a previous 50 per cent decline, those stocks didn't come close to regaining their former highs in the so-called bull market of May 1970 to January 1973. Instead, the rally was confined to those stocks favoured by institutional investors. After the market drop of 1969, the funds preferred issues that offered both liquidity and proven earnings growth, and that narrowed their field of choice down to a few hundred stocks. As a result, the market split into two tiers of stocks. One did in fact enjoy a run-up in 1972 and 1973. But the many, many stocks in the bottom tier sold at the lowest price-to-earnings ratios in twenty years.

In fact, the bull market of 1972 really existed only for those stocks favoured by the institutions. That explains why the Dow Jones and the S&P 500 indexes hit new highs that year while the average stock on the New York Stock Exchange as measured by the Value Line Average index (which is made up of about 1,500 stocks, 90 per cent of which are listed on the NYSE) was selling 40 per cent below its 1968 high.

While the popular-weighted indexes were forging ahead to new historic highs, two out of three stocks on the NYSE actually declined in price. For these stocks, which comprised the majority of the market, these years were nothing less than a correction within a severe bear market that started in 1969 and continued for six years. The decline during 1973 was especially harsh, and the average NYSE stock lost 75 per cent of its value. In all, total market value eroded by $360 billion, and the top fifty stocks accounted for $155 billion of that.

Equally depressing for stockholders was the fact that a massive sawtoothed pattern was traced out by the Dow during the 1970s. It was a "kangaroo market." There were three major, and one minor, declines, during which the investment scene resembled that of the 1930s. These were interspersed with powerful and sustained bull moves, when some of the old euphoria returned. The switches were confusing and sudden, and left analysts and brokers demoralized. Investors were whipsawed, and millions of them left the market, most never to return.

At first the declines seemed to be caused by the usual factors: excess speculation, weak brokerage firms, shaky businesses, tight money, recession, political leaders who had lost public trust. All these were familiar to old-timers and students of the market. But, above all, there was an ingrained fear of inflation. The consumer price index rose sharply in the early 1970s, its worst performance since the early postwar period.

When stock prices took off in the 1950s and then soared in the 1960s, it probably had more to do with investor psychology than with economic fundamentals. Improving sales, earnings, and dividends were present then, as they had been in the mid-1940s and the late 1970s, but the market did not behave as spectacularly in those periods. Their presence is necessary for a bull market, but they don't assure the development of a sustained bull market. For that, investors need to display boundless optimism and confidence in the future.

Such is the nature of market psychology that, in the middle of a major bull or bear phase, it is difficult to believe that the laws of the market really do apply. In his 1980 book *The Last Bull Market*, Robert Sobel wondered, in prefacing his study of the postwar bull market: Was this truly the last bull market this generation will know, or was it merely the last we had? Writing in 1980 he despaired of another one soon. (Of course, 1982 marked the start of the next one.) "Whatever happens," he lamented, "it is probable that there never again will be anything quite like this last bull market." Of course he was completely wrong, just as anyone will be who ventures the notion that the current bull will never again be matched.

What people tend to forget is that the laws of the market always apply.

One important tenet has to do with supply and demand. In the late summer of 1946, when the business outlook in the United States was more promising than it had been for some time, the stock market abruptly dropped 23 per cent. For the rest of the 1940s, the stock market moved sideways, an unusually prolonged period (it became known as the Sideways Market). The Dow bottomed out at 160 in 1949, a level below that of thirteen years earlier. Some analysts argued that stock prices were artificially depressed as a result of fears of a new depression and by political uncertainties, which discouraged the speculative short-term investor.

But there was more to it than that. At play was one of the major factors affecting primary movements in the market: the availability of money for stock investment. That is mainly affected by the attractiveness of competing investments, the size and distribution of the national income, and the availability of credit for stock purchases. As John Clendenin, a professor of finance at the University of California, Los Angeles, described in his 1964 book, *Introduction to Investments*, "The great bull market of 1927–1929 was aided by a national income distribution which favoured the well-to-do and middle-class professional men, who are likely stock buyers; by a high level of interest in stocks, which temporarily eclipsed life insurance and other outlets; and by the ready availability of margin credit, which enabled stock buyers to buy on credit to the extent of $9 billion. The contrast to the 1946–1949 situation is notable. Though the well-to-do and professional classes had satisfactory earnings in 1946–1949, high progressive taxes reduced their surpluses for investment to modest amounts, and the substantial incomes going to farmers and wage earners did not find their way into the stock market. Credit for the stock market was almost a thing of the past. And the 1946–1949 stock market did not advance despite prosperity, profits and dividends."

By contrast, the threefold advance in the Dow during the 1950s was due just as much to psychological and emotional factors as to economic ones. American confidence was buoyant again, running higher than it had since before the 1929 crash. Americans came to believe that prosperity was there to stay and that the political scene, both domestically and internationally, was in hand. The newly affluent middle class entered the stock market, many because they were free to do so after completing investments in their homes and family businesses. Americans were receptive to new sales pitches from Wall Street—

including a new investment vehicle, the mutual fund. Charles Merrill and his new breed of account executive fanned interest in the stock market across small-town America. Institutional investors, particularly corporate pension funds, also began to invest heavily in equities. Margin credit of 50 per cent became available. And new stocks made their appearance, providing the market with a touch of glamour and excitement, which is also a necessary ingredient for any sustained and spectacular move upward. Despite a generally lacklustre earnings picture—especially in 1954 and 1958—share prices were exploded.

From 1949 on, the Dow rose from a low of 262 to a peak of 685. Millions were made on Wall Street in the 1950s. Confidence, greed, and speculation surfaced. Fears of a crash like the one in 1929 at long last faded.

By 1959, a majority of shareholders had undergone their first investment experience during the second stage of the bull market. They hadn't been in the market at any time before, during, or immediately after the war, and many individual investors didn't buy stocks during the first big advance in the stock market from 1949 to 1953. But time was finally right. A forty-nine-year-old in 1959 would have been nineteen years of age in October 1929. He might have had friends or family who had lost money in the Great Crash, but it was unlikely he had experienced the trauma first-hand.

Like the market of the 1990s, the bull of the 1960s withstood frequent predictions by bears that it was coming to an end and frequent appearances of headlines like the one in *Business Week*, which wondered: "Where do we go from here? and answered "Higher, by most indications." This is reminiscent of the scene of the past few years in the stock market.

Inflationary pressure preoccupied the central bank, but good economic news, growing business confidence, and higher corporate earnings propelled stocks. Not all the bull-market sceptics were convinced. One mutual fund manager had worried that stock yields were very low and multiples quite high. Indeed, the Dow's multiple was almost 19; a year earlier it had been 16. On the other hand, bullish analysts noted, the price-to-earnings multiple had been as high as 24 only a few years before—implying that the market had a long way to go before topping out. And, they said, the yield factor was no longer very important. This Time It's Different.

By the mid-1960s inflation was on the rise and the market was behaving erratically. *Barron's* columnist Alan Abelson saw signs of a topping-out process (just as he has for the past couple of years on the 1990s bull). "With its strong speculative tinge, the market for some weeks hasn't been exactly suited for widows and orphans. Nor is it likely to become so in the foreseeable future." At about that time, the Dow had shot up more in two and half months than it had in all of 1964.

Typical of the late stages of a bull market, investors began taking profits in the decade's high-flying glamour stocks—such as National Video and Electrographic, little-known issues that had skyrocketed in price while the blue-chips struggled—and turned their interest to the safer blue-chip issues. Many of them were stocks of companies involved directly or indirectly with government spending, especially defence-related, construction, and new technologies, such as AT&T, General Electric, Westinghouse, Pan Am, and glamour stocks like Control Data and Teledyne; without the demand of the Cold War, IBM could not have grown as rapidly as it did.

The market of the mid to late 1960s has some striking similarities to the current one. Throughout this period, the market gyrated between sharp declines and rallies, and the Dow attempted to break past 1000 a number of times. By 1965 a small number of analysts thought a correction overdue. They warned that the price-to-earnings ratios of many leading issues were out of line with economic reality, and worried about the prospects for corporate profits. One brokerage firm declared: "It would take a blind man not to notice the many signs that have presented themselves which have been typical of the last stages in past major bull markets—pronounced profit-taking in high flyer, glamour stocks; renewed interest in safer blue chip issues ..." A number of big mutual funds such as the Dreyfus Fund accumulated $100 million in cash as a precaution. But none of the bears looked at a larger picture of budgetary deficits, the gold situation, and the declining dollar, and thought they were cause for a serious decline.

In the end, however, the bull market did top, and then turned because of factors not much occupying the minds of investors and market strategists of the day: namely, an end to the U.S. dollar's position as a store of value, which the U.S. had enjoyed since the end of the war, along with a deepening involvement in Vietnam. As it turned out, these two forces were interrelated, and each possessed a psychological as well as an economic dimension. Together these forces overwhelmed the bullishness of the market.

Edson Gould of Arthur Wiesenberger, a leading market theoretician, analysed the psychology of the market in the face of growing economic strains and a changing national mood regarding Vietnam. In late December 1965, he wrote that the Dow could move as high as 1140 to 1160 in the spring, but then decline sharply, perhaps as low as 650. He based this on his technical studies, the money supply, and very little else. His words apply today: "Unfortunately, market projections are not that simple. Also, monetary factors are just one of the variables in the stock market equation. Equally important—especially at major stock market peaks—are the psychological factors. And economic factors are always important; some imbalances in the economy always make their appearance prior to a major market peak."

In the thick of it, as the bull market played out, Wall Street was more concerned with the much-hyped debut of Gerry Tsai's Manhattan Fund and the significance of a Dow at 1000 as a major psychological barrier. The thinking was that, if the market could push through confidently, there was no reason why the index wouldn't continue its rise. But if the market faltered, a correction was possible—"the unraveling of a self-fueling prophecy," as Sobel has put it. All this, of course, was a matter of emotion rather than economics. We know now that the peak of that bull market was in February 1966, when, with the ticker tapes running late, the Dow hit an intraday high of 1001.11. Seven years later, it again hit 1000, but that was measured in dollars ravaged by the inflation of the 1970s.

All attempts to extend the bull failed. Some blue-chips reported good earnings and raised their dividends, and their stock prices fell anyway. There were no signs of a faltering economy, yet stock prices declined at an accelerating pace. Morgan Guaranty raised its prime lending rate to a level not seen since the 1930s. Fears of inflation surfaced. Funds with large cash positions, like Dreyfus, weren't buying. They preferred prudence—and liquidity. But the big portfolios were hamstrung: With hundreds of millions of dollars of blue-chip stocks, they couldn't sell even a fraction of these holdings into a weak market without setting off a major panic. The net effect was that, throughout 1966, the market steadily drifted lower, even though most economic signs were good.

"Had the great bull market finally ended?" wrote Sobel in his book. "There was little talk of this in the press, the business magazines or the brokerages. So powerful and prolonged an upward move hardly could be concluded by a simple decline on low volume, said Wall Street veterans, and they noted that obituaries had been released during similar corrections in 1953, 1957, 1962 and as recently 1965. They were not prepared to write off this bull market unless and until it reached a dramatic climax similar to that of 1929, and in the early autumn of 1966 this didn't seem possible."

Whenever markets are analysed, we use as our guide what has been. The bull market of the 1920s was climaxed by the Great Depression. The 1960s ended with the Great Inflation. Those who had lived through the Dirty Thirties easily recognized the hallmarks of depression: lost jobs, wage cuts, foreclosures, and shrinking savings.

With the inflationary era, losses were more difficult to discern. Often they appeared to be gains. Only over time did investors come to see this, and over time they departed the stock market, using their money to buy bonds or consumer goods. The great bull of the 1950s and 1960s came to a conclusion, not with the dramatic crash of the 1920s, where fortunes were wiped out overnight, but with a quiet and prolonged undermining.

The market of the 1960s did have one last blowout, and the Dow peaked at 994 in December 1968. It was led by a mania for new issues, small esoteric companies, and over-the-counter stocks. Investors, many of them new to the market, clamoured for such things as chicken franchises and aquaculture stocks—and the mutual fund industry obliged with new "ocean technology" funds. There was also a mania for mergers and hostile takeovers.

Despite the strong evidence that there was very little left in the bull, small-time investors climbed aboard anyway. There were 15 per cent more shareholders in 1968 than there had been two years earlier. Trading was so frantic that, at one point, a famous event now, the stock exchanges began closing on Wednesday afternoons so that brokerage firms could catch up on their paperwork. A seat on the NYSE changed hands for a record amount of money. New mutual funds were starting up at a rate of one a week in 1968, and most of them were "performance oriented." Funds flowed in from European money markets, pushing up the Dow as overseas buyers lapped up some $1.3 billion in U.S. stocks. (A recurrent and familiar theme of stock markets over the nineteenth and twentieth centuries has been the appearance of foreign buyers at precisely the point when American markets are set to top.)

When interest rates were hiked unexpectedly at the end of 1968, the Dow plunged. Within a year and a half, almost one-third of the index's value melted away, even while people talked of a possible upturn in the early 1970s. It took a long time for the reality of a bear market to sink in. In the fallout, proposed mergers never happened, new issues disappeared, and most of the "go-go" mutual funds closed down.

Harry Schultz, writing in the early 1960s, skewered popular delusions of his day, and in doing so said something that applies equally today. "In every age there are people who claim, 'This couldn't happen today.' People are saying it now, that this is a new age of prosperity. Yet they were saying that in 1929. During the 1929–32 period, Standard Oil fell to 50, at which point the Rockefellers felt it had fallen far enough so they 'pegged' it at 50 by buying gobs of its. The piece held together for a while. But by the end of the bear market, it had fallen to 20! U.S. Steel fell from 626 to 22. General Motors collapsed from 73 to 8. Montgomery Ward 'dropped dead' from 138 to 4. AT&T suffered from a high of 304 to 72. If we think it can't happen again, we are merely hoping. It not only can happen again, but it can be worse.

"Again I am told by long-time investors that 'they always come back.' They advise me with a condescending expression that I can just 'buy and hold,' because in time 'they all come back again.' The man who said this was just then seeing his Royal Dutch return to what he paid for it seven years ago."

The growing faith in the long-term advantage of equities coincided with the rise of the institutional investors. By the early 1970s the funds had amassed huge holdings in blue-chip stocks which could not be liquidated easily. These stocks, the "Nifty Fifty," were called "one-decision" stocks—you make the decision to buy them and that was it—and included Polaroid, General Electric, Procter & Gamble. Their prices held up through the early part of the early 1970s bear because they were so popular with the institutions, who had a voracious appetite for them. As a result, two tiers formed in the market: While the overall market got the jitters, the Nifty Fifty stayed fairly solid. However, over the course of 1974, the value of the Dow dropped 50 per cent and that meltdown took the Nifty Fifty with it. The long-established notion that stocks and bond prices behaved inversely fell apart.

While the postwar bull ended differently from the bull of the Roaring '20s, there are two great crashes from which to draw some knowledge, 1929 and 1987. They were of similar scale—the Dow fell 12.8 per cent on October 18, 1929, and another 11.7 per cent the following day, for a combined decline of 23 per cent. On October 19, 1987, the market plummeted 22.5 per cent in one day. And in both cases the market had already turned down a few weeks ahead of the big meltdown.

The consensus among most economists and historians now is that the root cause of the 1929 crash was the use of low margins. Stock speculators of the time could put as little as 10 per cent down on their investments. When the market began to drop and the margin calls came, not only were most people wiped out, but the extent of the free-fall was exacerbated as brokers sold out their clients in order to meet margin calls.

By 1987, the individual was certainly no longer the dominating presence in the market—having been supplanted by the institution. And margins were limited to 50 per cent. But those pension funds and mutual funds had dreamed up "portfolio insurance," a computerized technique involving hedging the market indexes as a way of protecting portfolios in a falling market but which had the effect of vastly acceler- ating a market crash because the computer programs triggered a cascade of sell orders.

The lessons of history are more difficult to discern from the aftermath of the two crashes. The grinding depression that followed the Crash of '29 likely was as deep and protracted as it was because of errors in the government's management of the economy. That's what most historians believe; however, there are some who think the evaporation of wealth that resulted from the crash was a major reason for the terrible years that followed.

By contrast, the 1987 market débâcle had little effect on the economy. The stock market quickly bounced back to pre-crash levels, and a recession did not appear until three years after the meltdown. One reason was that the U.S. central bank drowned the economy in money. For another, the impact on individuals was more muted because, at the time, households had a larger stake in real estate than they did in the stock market. Today the opposite is true, and American and Canadian households have more in stocks than property.

Anyone who argues that the past has little relevance to today's bull market because This Time It's Different might consider the following two passages. The parallels with today are obvious.

"By the summer of 1929 the market not only dominated the news. It also dominated the culture," wrote John Kenneth Galbraith in *The Great Crash*. "That recherché minority which at other times has acknowledged its interest in St. Thomas Aquinas, Proust, psychoanalysis and psychosomatic medicine then spoke of United Founders & Steel ... Main Street had always had one citizen who could speak knowingly about buying and selling stocks. Now he had become an oracle."

"Growth took on an almost mystical significance," wrote Burton Malkiel of the early 1960s in *A Random Walk on Wall Street*, "and questioning the propriety of such valuations became, as in the generation past, almost heretical. These prices could not be justified on firm foundation principles."

Finally, in February of this year, U.S. Federal Reserve Board chairman Alan Greenspan made public remarks aimed at talking down the roaring stock market, without actually breaking it. He spoke of the irrationality and optimism and delusions of investors. Stock holders responded by shrugging off his remarks, but the lesson of history is: Ignore his warnings at your peril.

Before Greenspan made his remarks in February (and in a previous speech in December 1996), there were only two other instances when the Fed had made a similar attempt to curb the stock market. In the 1920s the Fed was a far weaker and less prestigious entity than it is now, but a statement issued in February 1929 tried to get banks to stop borrowing from the Fed at low interest rates and then lending the money to speculators in the stock market. For a time the Dow declined slightly, but then went on to peak later that year. In June 1965, then-Fed chair, William McChesney Martin, Jr. gave a speech referring to "disquieting similarities between our present prosperity and the fabulous 20s." Although he did not directly comment on stock prices, stocks sold off, and by the time the market bottomed nearly a month later, the Dow was down 8.4 per cent. A rally then ensued, until prices peaked eight months after Martin had spoken, with the Dow just under 1000, and 8.4 per cent higher than that June. It was not until 1982 that the Dow topped 1000 for good.

CHAPTER SIX

Survival Strategies:
The Case for Selling Too Soon

*"There are no great problems in a bull market; all one
has to do is buy good stocks and sit. A bear market,
however, is a treacherous thing, offering unlimited
opportunities for losing money."*

—FORBES, JULY 15, 1962

I started investing in stocks in 1974 in the depths of a vicious bear
market. The Dow's low in December of that year was 570, half of
what it had been in the late 1960s. As I write this in early 1997, the
Dow is above 7000. It has been a hell of a good ride, and any investor
would have to be stupid not to have made money during this time. In
a bull market, the trend is up, after all, and a rising tide floats all boats—
an overused aphorism, perhaps, but very true in this case.

During the 1980s and 1990s, no one needed to be brilliant or perceptive or in possession of extraordinary intelligence to be successful
with stocks. In fact, forget about investment strategies and portfolio
management: All you had to do was buy the index averages and you
could make fourteen times your money.

Most people nonetheless mistake good fortune for financial brilliance and make an erroneous connection between money and intelligence. In his book *A Short History of Financial Euphoria*, John
Kenneth Galbraith notes that "the investing public is fascinated and
captured by the great financial mind. That fascination derives, in turn,

from … the feeling that, with so much money involved, the mental resources behind them cannot be less. Only after the speculative collapse does the truth emerge. What was thought to be unusual acuity turns out to be only a fortuitous and unfortunate association with the assets."

Nearly everyone in today's stock market—amateurs and professionals alike—secretly or not so secretly believes he (or she) has a special prowess that serves him well in his investments. Experts and gurus have loaded up the investor with all sorts of advice. Buy the stocks of companies you know from your daily life. (Thus, according to Robert Prechter, Jr., McDonald's is the number-one stock by a long shot of amateur investment clubs.) Pick a handful of "good stocks" and stick by them. Hold for the long term.

The thing is, almost any method or theory will work in a bull market, particularly one as long in duration as the one we have had for the past fifteen years. Most investors today are well trained and they don't know how to behave any other way. Like Pavlov's dogs, they act automatically: Buy in the sell-offs; hold for the long term. They know for sure that stocks only go up.

But lessons learned in the great bull market have little value in any other kind of market environment; you need different skills for adapting to a new market condition. Most important, to survive a big bear you must unlearn everything you've learned during your investing career—and this is not a simple matter.

Unfortunately, there is no road map. Most stock market advice is about optimism, not pessimism, and about buying, not selling. Look in the library or bookstore for advice on how to survive a bear and you won't find it. The stock market and its practitioners, supporters, and observers make their living from being in the market, not out of it. Most investors, whether the professional manager with the $5-billion pension fund or the individual with a retirement savings account, have little knowledge and even less experience with bears, or "panics," as they once were known.

First, let's analyse the current situation: the coming end of a bull market.

Heightened activity in the market is very typical of the bull's final stages: Normally there are vast gyrations in price, and great rotation among stocks, as investors chase ever-higher returns and become more difficult to satisfy. The first stocks to rise in a bull—consumer goods, food, pharmaceuticals—have already moved up substantially. The rewards have mainly been taken, and so their price appreciation slows.

Demand for the shares of those large corporations starts to peter out as buyers move on to something else. Even if the earnings in those companies are up 25 to 30 per cent, they still will not meet the earnings *expectations* that have built up during the final phase of the bull.

To get the kind of returns they've become accustomed to, investors must move into lower-quality, riskier issues in faster-moving markets. This is why you find big-name funds buying stocks like Cartaway Resources and Bre-X.

Stock buyers also rapidly fall in and out of love with entire industry groups at the end of a market cycle. Thus, in early 1996 we saw investors move into smaller, less proven ventures in certain sectors: computer and Internet, biotech, and mineral exploration. That's why the Dow rose less in the first half of 1996 than the NASDAQ. The Vancouver Stock Exchange, an extremely speculative marketplace, doubled in the first half of 1996.

By this point, analysts are usually overestimating their earnings forecasts. The bar has been raised. And the market is setting itself up for disappointment—and a sell-off.

For the inevitable result, look what happened to those high-flying technology stocks in the second half of 1996—a massive meltdown across the board, with anywhere from one-third to two-thirds of a stock's value wiped out in the short course of a month or so as portfolio managers dumped the sector en masse and moved on.

Of course, while they're doing the buying, most investors don't recognize the excessive risk they're taking. Even if they do, they are compelled to take the risk, especially if they are institutions who must try to outperform their competitors and the market if they are to continue to attract new money (if they are mutual funds) or keep their clients (if they are pension funds). Once again, we have those basic market emotions—greed and fear—kicking in.

The last group to move in a bull are the cyclicals: mining, commodities, steel, and transportation. By mid-1996, these were the favourites in the Canadian and U.S. markets. After the excitement of the small-cap stocks, the pendulum swings back to the blue-chips, led by the consumer-group and the large-cap stocks, which are deemed significantly "safer" than the small-caps.

This goes on until that group of stocks reaches an overbought level and the investors who were in earliest unload their stocks onto the last ones in. The whole thing is like a game of musical chairs, where the last in is without a seat. It is the "greater fool" theory: You buy a stock—no matter how overpriced—on the expectation that there will be somebody else to buy it from you.

How should an individual play this phase? Easy. You stay in the rotation game. Mutual funds, which are playing the game on your behalf, are in the market to the end and they make extremely good money in the final phase of a bull.

But be clear that mutual funds are downgrading their holdings at this point. It's the old formula: increased reward equals increased risk. The market will reward fund managers for a while with higher quarterly and annualized rates of returns. But the process eventually comes to an end, and the high risk of those lower quality holdings can overnight become no reward, or huge losses.

Naturally, mutual fund managers are convinced that they're smart enough to get out by the time the music stops. Perhaps they have forgotten the words of that great Wall Street figure of the 1920s and 1930s, Bernard Baruch: "Don't try to buy at the bottom and sell at the top. This can't be done—except by liars." Baruch sold his stockholdings before the Crash of '29.

To be fair, most managers have very little choice about staying in the market until it turns. (If you are nervous about your fund staying in, think about switching to a fund with greater leeway in keeping a large proportion of the fund in cash.) Their mandate is to be fully invested, and their cash positions can be only a small part of the total portfolio. Meanwhile, money keeps pouring in from the public and it has to go somewhere. Stocks, no matter how ominous the signs in the market, are their only option.

It's worth recalling how institutional money managed to keep the Nifty Fifty afloat in the late 1960s and early 1970s. As I mentioned previously, the Nifty Fifty stocks (such as IBM, Xerox, and Polaroid) were relatively untouched by the decline in 1966–68 as compared with what happened to most stocks trading on the New York Stock Exchange and NASDAQ.

Today our version of the Nifty Fifty stocks includes McDonald's, Coca-Cola, AT&T, BCE, Northern Telecom, and the five big Canadian banks. They sat out much of the craziness of 1996, as evidenced by the 1990s glamour stocks—the technologies, the minerals, and the "concepts." But when the institutions start to sell stocks, we will see the market decline rapidly accelerate. Once the fund managers believe the bull is over and the débâcle has begun, they will sell their core positions. Watch out when that happens!

Galbraith's rules for remedying the recurrent descent into insanity, which, as he put it, "is not a wholly attractive feature of capitalism," are worth examining:

First, maintain an enhanced scepticism that would resolutely—one might also add, routinely—associate too much optimism with probable foolishness. Second, when a mood of excitement pervades a market or surrounds an investment prospect, or when there is a claim of unique opportunity based on special foresight, it is a time for caution. Finally, he writes, "there is the possibility and even the likelihood of self-approving and extravagantly error-prone behavior on the part of those closely associated with money."

If ever there was a stock to prove these rules it is Bre-X Minerals. The hype that drove that company's shares from pennies to well over a hundred dollars (before splitting) emanated solely from the men running the company—and yet everyone had no trouble believing their extraordinary claims of having the richest gold find on the planet, some 200 million ounces. The financial analysts also believed religiously in the company's statements, and they set values uncritically, without taking into consideration that the property was in high-risk Indonesia. It was a story to good to be true, and almost everyone did believe.

How to Survive

Despite the busy punditry industry in the investment world, nobody can really forecast the market on a short-term basis. Nobody can tell you what the market will do next week or next month, or often even next year. According to the Dow Theory, "neither the duration nor extent of a primary move can be predicted in advance." But we can paint a bigger picture for you, based on our knowledge of the past, and tell you what the market will do when the big turn comes.

You can learn what can happen, even though you might not know exactly when it will happen. You can be given the warning signals and the general knowledge that this turn will take place in the next twelve to eighteen months, and you can prepare yourself.

It gives you the means to protect yourself and, most important, it gives you time to make a decision in advance of moment-to-moment events.

Most bad decisions happen during a panic. And most people tend to freeze in a panic.

I am very good under pressure—that's the only reason I have survived so long as a trader. This is my approach: I decide what's real or when it will become real. To protect myself, I usually have limits. I have an automatic stop-loss with my broker on the trades I make, so that I don't have to pick up the phone. In a panic you will find your friendly mutual fund salesman or stockbroker is unavailable. The telephone rings, but no one answers, or you get a busy signal. This is exactly what happened during the market meltdown of October 1987. And minutes count in such a situation. So always make advance arrangements.

So here we have the high probability that a big bear is set to come ambling onto North American equity markets sometime in the near term. So what should you do?

That depends on your individual circumstances: your age, the extent of your stockholdings, the degree of your reliance on funds for retirement. It also depends on your time-frame—how close you are to retirement.

Here are two rules for everybody, whatever their circumstances:

Rule # 1: Don't buy at the top, no matter how many friends brag about the return on their mutual funds.

The best time to buy stocks is when interest rates are high and experts declare that stocks just can't compete with bonds or bank deposits. The question to ask yourself is this: Did you have the courage to buy stocks in the mid-1980s, when such conditions existed? If you didn't, then you should not be buying stocks at current exorbitant prices in 1997.

The right approach as prices near the peak of a bull market is to use the time you have to liquidate your equity investments and shift your money into interest-bearing investments or specialty funds.

Rule # 2: You cannot expect to make money in a bear market. The name of the game is to preserve capital, earn a modest return, and have your capital available when the bear market is over.

The issue is not who will make the most, but who will lose the least. Those who lose the least will have kept their money liquid and safe from the storm.

Keep in mind that, on a long-term basis, stocks always outperform any other instrument—whether it's a 100-year, 60-year or 30-year time-frame.

The well-respected Florida-based statistician Ned Davis provides some fascinating analysis: From 1926 to 1995, the S&P 500 returned 10.4 per cent a year. U.S. government bonds returned 5 per cent a year, U.S. Treasury bills 3.9 per cent a year, inflation averaged 3.1 per cent. Of the S&P's return, 40 per cent of it came from dividends. But returns from the period 1985 to 1995 show a far different result. The S&P returned 14.3 per cent a year during that time, but the annual average yield was much lower, around 3.3 per cent, while price appreciation was much higher. Given that the sixty-nine years incorporated the highs and lows of booms, depressions, and wars, one could take that as the "norm." So, if the past ten-year return is so much higher, it can only portend a return to the norm—via a major price decline.

The point is twofold: I believe in the long run you should be able to make good money under any conditions in the marketplace. Statistics show that, over the long term, stocks do outperform bonds. And when inflation is taken into account, bonds and other interest-bearing investments can actually cost you money.

However, timing is everything.

In the short term—say, five to ten years—stocks can be very dangerous. Buy stocks at the wrong time in the market cycle—in a full-blown speculative bubble such as we have had—and you can lose much of your capital. This is what market timing is all about: where you get into the market and where you get out.

There are two ways to tackle the timing issue.

One is to dollar-cost average your mutual fund investments. Putting in a certain amount regularly from every paycheque every week or every month means that you are buying through highs and lows, dips and tops. For younger people that is most definitely the way to go.

The second way—and the point of this book—is to do some macro-style market timing.

In the short term, there are times when disaster strikes with special severity. Bonds can produce a huge *negative* rate of return in the short term. The year 1994 was a good example: The depreciation on the bond values was 22 per cent, as the interest rate reached about 8 per cent (up from 6 per cent). Therefore if you held a long-term bond from the top to the bottom you would have lost 16 per cent. If you were lucky, you did not get out at the bottom (in November) but rather held on until December 1995—when, if you sold, you "only" lost about 8 per cent—not 16 per cent.

Obviously, you should diversify your portfolio not only in terms of the types of investment vehicles, but also geographically. Whether you are a U.S. or Canadian citizen, if you have had all of your nest eggs in one basket and that basket was the North American market, this was your greatest blessing for the past century. Virtually no country has outperformed North American equity markets during this period. But what was true for the past century may not be true for the next.

Since 1968, Japan has significantly outperformed the North

American stock market. Both the Dow Jones and the Nikkei were at 1000 in 1968. However, the Tokyo index reached 38957 by 1990 (before its free-fall to 14200), while the Dow Jones merely quadrupled, to 4000 and reached 5800 by mid-1996. The "Tigers"—South Korea, Taiwan, Hong Kong, Singapore, and Indonesia—grew almost 10 per cent per annum over the past fifteen to twenty years, and the stock markets there have also outperformed North America during that time. However, there are volatile fluctuations and great political risks in the region, and also a significant scarcity of liquidity. Individual investors can't participate in those markets as freely as in North America. That, plus a lack of skill and knowledge of the investment scene there, makes it unrealistic to expect that any individual could really play those stock markets in preference to the one at home.

For most people, diversification has meant having a broader list of stocks spread among industries, markets, long-term, short-term, fixed income, common shares, value stocks or growth stocks, dividend-paying, and no-dividend. (Keep in mind, however, that indexed funds such as the S&P 500 and the TSE 300 outperform two-thirds or more of the mutual funds and money managers. If you have nothing but S&P 500 index funds and you hold them over a long period of time, you will not do any worse than mutual funds and you don't have to pay management fees or transaction costs.)

Strategies

Obviously, what you do in preparation for the coming bear depends on your age and your needs for retirement. If you have twenty or more years to retirement, then by all means pack your portfolio with equities. A thirty-year-old who invests money on a gradual basis every year—say, $10,000 or so—for a thirty-year term, has very little to worry about in a typical bear market. When you are buying stocks on the instalment plan, you can also buy some of the more aggressive funds because you get more bang for your buck on the volatility. Even with more conservative funds, dollar-cost averaging reduces the risk of the market by almost one-third, according to some reputable studies. Mutual fund managers will use your regular contributions to buy cheaper stocks. But don't count on a rapid turn-around. Don't forget: Investors who bought General Motors in 1929 didn't see the same price until 1950.

But if you had bought stock at the peak in 1929 and then continued to contribute all through the decline and subsequent doldrums, by 1950 you were way ahead because of dollar averaging and dividend income. On the other hand, if you had taken your money out prior to the crash and reinvested it after 1932 when the worst was over, you would have made more than 300 per cent.

What about the fifty-five- or sixty-year-old, close to retirement, and with a sizeable portfolio of investments to protect? You absolutely do not want to leave it to the vagaries of the market. The closer you get to retirement, the more you should limit the common-share proportion of your portfolio and the more you should build up other components. If your nest egg is in mutual funds, and your plan is to start cashing in four or five years hence, then a vicious bear market could reduce your million-dollar nest egg to $600,000 five years down the road. For the next couple of years, that is a very real possibility—far greater than the possibility that the $1 million could grow by another $200,000. With the odds so much against you, there is very little reason to take such a chance so close to retirement. Any loss of capital at this stage cannot be made back. It is far better to be satisfied with a lower rate of return on a GIC or Treasury bill than risk losing that capital.

For those approaching age sixty, I would suggest that you move a substantial portion—certainly more than half and perhaps as much as three-quarters—of your assets out of equities. Nearing age sixty-five, even more should be moved out of the stock market. That would leave you with at most 20 to 25 per cent in stocks. Then, even if you lose half in a bear market, you will still retain almost 90 per cent of your hard-won assets. More likely, you would lose one-third of your equity portfolio and, if you live long enough, even that will come back. Just as important is what kind of equities you should retain in that much-reduced portfolio and the safety of the investments you keep in your fixed-income portion.

For those aged fifty-five-plus, who have enjoyed a fifteen-year bull run and have seen a market rise of 1,000 per cent, it is only logical to take your profits, even though it may be painful to walk away from the 10 to 20 per cent that you're "sure" is left in the bull. Take advantage of your luck and cash in some of your chips. Put your assets into safe, income-producing investments, three- to five-year GICs or shorter renewable terms. If you have to live on your income in your retirement, my suggestion is that you must get out at this phase of the market. At this stage, it is not the accumulation but the preservation of wealth that should be your primary concern. Keep your money when all about you are losing theirs.

Now, if the stock market was at the bottom rather than the top, that would not be my recommendation to you. Then, I would say it is a great time to hold and see it appreciate. But with a major top forming, you cannot take that risk.

It is very difficult to make back lost savings, so your number-one goal is to keep your capital safe. Remember Warren Buffett's words: The first rule is not to lose your capital. The second rule is not to forget the first rule.

To do that, though, means you will be battling your emotions. Because, above all, whether the stock market is going up or down, it is ruled by emotions, and those two ruling emotions are, of course, fear and greed. Winning in the market is a matter of fighting a battle within yourself: intellect over emotion. Most people will lose that battle.

Knowing when to sell is just as important as knowing when to buy, but it is more difficult because we are dealing with opposites. Newsletter pundit Harry D. Schultz, in a book on bear markets he wrote in the 1960s, wisely said: "The act of staying out is just as much a positive action as buying or selling and in fact requires more courage at times." Then he quoted Robert Rhea, who said during the 1937 bear market: "A bear market is a good time for a vacation, and I am taking one."

So the most important factor is a psychological one: Change your outlook on how to react to market moves.

Fourteen or more years in a bull market teaches you to view every sell-off as a buying opportunity. Corrections become one of the market's greatest benefits because *you just know* it will always come back and move even higher. You know this because it has happened dozens of times before, and the market has trained us well. But that doesn't happen in a bear market. The trend has changed; it's headed downward and you need to learn a different, cautious game to protect yourself. A primary rule of the market is *never go against the trend.* That applies whether you are long or short. In a bear, if the number of new highs does not significantly exceed the number of new lows, you will be tempted to rationalize this away by saying something like, "The market's well down from its peak so it's to be expected." Wrong.

Every market rise in a bear market is an opportunity to sell. You are playing from the short side of the market in a bear—just as you played from the long side in the bull. "Averaging down in a bear market is tantamount to taking a seat on the down escalator at Macy's," Richard Russell wrote in his *Dow Theory Letters* in 1984.

The unassailable fact is, the character of the market has changed dramatically. In a bull market, the market moves generally on an upward slope, with sudden drops interspersed through the advance. In a bull market, this is a continuous process: The drops appear very frightening, but then they are relatively fast in reversing themselves.

In a bear market, the slope is generally downward, and the moves up are very dramatic, unexpected, and large. If you didn't get out before the crest, the top of a secondary rise in most bear markets offers the best prices you're likely to see for some time. Emotionally, you will feel you should have sold earlier (true) and that it is "too late" to sell now (not true). These are the best prices you can hope for, even though they are a major disappointment compared with prices of, say, six months earlier.

As the bear proceeds over time, it grinds down the natural optimism of investors: they get discouraged. The continuous decline ultimately has the effect of reducing—if not eradicating—the desire to buy. Volume is low and lacklustre, but there is also no great desire to sell because most of those who want to sell have already sold, and those who have not sold still cling to the hope that the market will turn.

It will not.

At the same time, there are those who go short. These are sophisticated investors. They believe they are playing the bear. But the short seller is the most faint-hearted of all those on the investment scene. The reason: When you go short there is no limit to what you can lose, unlike in long trades, where losses are limited to the value of the initial investment.

During the downward-sloping bear, the rapid up ticks indicate that the shorts are being squeezed and they are running for cover. They're trying to get out of the short positions (by buying stock) and that drives the market up. Once the shorts are all squeezed out, there are fewer moves upward. Professionals have many means of selling short, using derivatives, options, and puts. But even professionals get caught, and when a short goes wrong there is no limit to the loss, unlike a long position.

But what about prior to the start of the bear? If you're convinced it's coming, should you go short in a market that is trading at absurdly high price-to-earnings ratios on the assumption that a crash is coming? My answer is this: You have two choices, stay on the train or get off the train. But under no circumstances should you lie across the tracks. That's essentially what you would be doing by shorting in a bull market. It can kill you.

Other Markets

If you are wealthy—able to afford to lose some of your money—and you feel you *have* to be in the market and on the long side, what are your options?

Above all, keep in mind the risk-to-reward ratio, whatever the investment. That is a fundamental key to successful investing in any market. And it's not always as easy as it appears. For example, if you want to be out of the stock market, then bonds are an obvious alternative. However, if the economy succumbs to inflationary pressure, fixed income is no place to be. A rising-interest-rate environment would mean that long-term fixed-income instruments are very high risk and not a "safe" choice at all. On the other hand, if we end up dealing with deflation in our economy, they are the best investment to have.

Remember that diversification is important in ensuring that all of your investments do not go up or down at the same time. Asset allocation, as it is called, is always about risk management.

The attraction of an internationally diversified portfolio is that it will lead you away from the soon-to-be treacherous U.S. market. Participation in markets in South East Asia, South America, and Eastern Europe carry high risks, but they also will continue to produce much higher returns over the next few years. Of course, RRSP investors have to keep in mind Revenue Canada's rules governing the percentage of foreign equities (currently 20 per cent).

Already, investors who are wary of the bubble developing in the United States have been sinking their cash into diverse markets. In the tax-selling season in 1996, Americans poured $6.4 billion into international equity funds—almost as much as for the entire year of 1995. In Canada it was the same story: Investors piled $640 million into foreign market funds in January, a substantial increase over the $160 million a year earlier.

The trouble with this is that the same mania those investors are trying to escape in North America could be re-created overseas, largely because of the torrent of cash they bring with them. Cash, no matter where its destination, is still flowing recklessly into most markets.

Not that you can fault them. There is no guarantee that North America will continue to be *the* most attractive place to invest. The Far East, South America, Europe—they all offer tough competition. And if deflation, a devalued dollar, and taxation worry you, then moving some of your bets out of North America is wise. After all, the American dollar during the last twenty years has lost 5 per cent of its value per annum against the Deutschemark and the Japanese yen. The purchasing power of the dollar has declined more than 90 per cent since the end of the Second World War—something you only notice when you go to Europe and try to buy the same merchandise you can buy at home. In Switzerland, it costs more, and in Moscow, surprise, it will cost you even more. That doesn't mean that the dollar is not worth more than what it is able to buy. Its price is determined, not by its purchasing power domestically, but internationally. There are so many new dollars offered to the world, courtesy of the huge budget deficit and trade deficit (which add billions and billions of surplus dollars annually) that the world doesn't know what to do with them—except to devalue them.

The same applies to the Canadian dollar. And we in Canada have the misfortune of seeing our currency declining not only against the mark and the yen and the Swiss franc, but also against the U.S. dollar. When I came to Canada in 1957, one Canadian dollar bought four Swiss francs, four Deutschemarks, and 1.8 U.S. dollars. Today, one Canadian dollar gets you 1.1 Swiss francs, one Deutschemark, and 0.74 U.S. dollars. Again, the Canadian dollar's purchasing power around the world is devalued because of budgetary deficits.

During the past eighteen months the American dollar has appreciated against the mark, the Swiss franc, and the yen by more than 30 per cent. However, the G7 powerbrokers will have to put an end to this. My feeling is that the strength of the U.S. dollar over the last year or so will not continue. But, even if it does, it is prudent to maintain some balance of holdings in other currencies. My advice is to put one-third in U.S. currency, one-third in Canadian (for Canadian investors), and the balance in Swiss francs or yen.

These investments could be limited to currencies, where a Canadian could buy Government of Canada bonds denominated in U.S. dollars or German marks or yen. You could similarly buy Ontario Hydro bonds or Province of Ontario bonds.

You can buy multinational companies located in North America—you may feel more comfortable because you know them better—that do business internationally. If you own Coca-Cola, Ford, or Bombardier, you have international exposure. If you own commodity companies where international supply and demand determines commodity prices, then you have international exposure. But you should also aim to have sufficient participation in the rapid growth of the emerging economies of Asia, South America, and certain parts of Europe.

Even if foreign securities decline, the exchange-rate differential can result in an increase for you because of the currency appreciation.

That said, international diversification is not easy. Out there in the world market, you know less about where to invest, which industries, which companies, and following these markets is extremely difficult. The only way to overcome this tremendous disadvantage is to buy through mutual funds. I sincerely believe that the individual Canadian investor should have a third of his or her assets in Canada, a third in the United States, and the balance outside North America, roughly half in Europe and half in the Far East. An American should have 60 to 66 per cent in the U.S. markets, and the balance overseas. Historically, there has usually been a time lag before the Canadian markets follow the U.S. markets into a new bull market, and a delay before the Canadian markets follow the American markets into a bear. However, today, when Wall Street coughs, Bay Street gets pneumonia. With so many companies interlisted, and with communications and technology so profoundly changed since the last big market turn, the delay factor will not be very significant in practical terms.

Emerging markets, of course, hold the allure of rapid growth. Nowhere is that more likely than in South East Asia and China, which will continue to be the greatest place for growth in the world. Indonesia, China, South Korea, and Vietnam top the list. These markets are very investor-friendly but carry great political risks. China is doing the transition from communism much better than the ex–Soviet Union by concentrating fully on the creation of a market economy under strong centralized Communist Party control. Up to now it has succeeded. But no one can give you the assurance that China's political stability can be preserved. There are hundreds of millions of peasants living in poverty in the interior, whereas the wealth is concentrated in coastal areas. Can China's leaders avoid civil unrest, the emergence of local warlords, or a challenge to the military dictatorship? The hope—where investors are concerned—is that they will; the risk is that they won't.

Meanwhile, the likelihood is that other countries in the region will follow suit, likely Vietnam, and most likely the Philippines. Probably the richest country will be Indonesia, with its tremendous known resources in oil, gold, minerals, lumber, and food, but we have already learned the hard way about doing business there.

The only way for the public to participate in this is with emerging market funds. Just make sure the fund is competently managed and go for the big names, such as Templeton, Fidelity, Vanguard, Alliance, and J.P. Morgan.

Latin America is my other recommendation. I like the prospects in Argentina, Chile, and Brazil. Mexico, despite all the problems, and there are huge problems, could be a dark horse. Remember, the United States has to solve Mexico's problems because, if it doesn't, illegal immigration will not only continue, but escalate, threatening major cities such as New York and Houston. Americans can't afford that.

Chile is probably the most developed economy in South America. I believe Argentina is going to be the next one. Demand for agricultural exports is rising, and the investment environment is improving—so much so that I predict there will be a new boom once the multinationals are attracted. Those countries have tremendous natural resources, especially known reserves of oil, gold, and minerals. All that's required is the capital to exploit them—and the means.

Brazil is probably one of the richest countries on the planet. The country has huge industry, huge agriculture, mining, power sources, and an unexplored interior. What the country lacks is political stability, an educated labour force, and population control. I believe the last fifty years have created an economic base which one day will explode and move Brazil up to the top of the industrialized countries. But there is one thing: It needs to resolve the problem of the huge disparity between the rich and the poor or the inflationary danger and the threat of social unrest will be real and continuous—and that will suppress the country's entire stock market.

The question for investors venturing outside of North America of course is this: When the U.S. market does turn down, will it affect foreign stock markets? If the crash of 1987 is any indication, then the answer is yes. In 1987 the massive drop in the Dow triggered similar dives in every market around the globe within twenty-four hours. It was like a set of dominoes falling. But it was not felt to the same extent elsewhere. When the Dow Industrials plummeted 23 per cent in one day, in October 1987, the next day Tokyo's market fell 15 per cent and then resumed its powering up to a bull-market top two years later.

Similarly, market rises are not uniformly felt around the globe. In 1993, the Morgan Stanley Capital International's EAFE Index (Europe, Australasia, and Far East) rocketed 30.5 per cent while the S&P climbed only 10 per cent. The Japanese market boomed when the U.S. market was in its longest bear phase, 1968–82. The Japanese market went into a vicious bear phase in 1990, while the U.S. market had its strongest bull run.

Speaking of Japan, it was once the hottest investment in South East Asia, but it has been a no man's land for investors during its tussle with that tremendous bear beginning in 1990. The Nikkei index went from just under 40,000 to 14,000 points in mid-1995—a 64 per cent drop. Since then it has experienced a significant recovery to 22,000 over the last two years, better than a 50 per cent rise.

The severe decline is over. The economic outlook in Japan is somewhat improved. For 1996, Japan grew 3.5 per cent, compared with the 1 per cent growth rate previously expected. Japanese corporations, whose exports were hamstrung by a strong yen, have recently benefited from a devaluation of the yen against the U.S. dollar and the German mark. As the many Japanese companies dependent on export markets begin showing improved earnings, stock prices have started to respond.

I believe it will decline somewhat again, and that will be a good opportunity to purchase shares in the Japanese market.

The Japanese economy is undergoing a major, wrenching transition, and growth for 1997 will probably be only 1.5 per cent. The bursting of the 1980s bubble economy led to a severe recession, the worst for the country since the Second World War. Domestically, competition is going to be felt for the first time in Japan since the war in many fields, which will allow the Japanese consumer to purchase more and consume more and save at the same time. The yen has declined to a very attractive rate, which should help exports. The Japanese tradition of maintaining staff forever was shattered by the recession.

Japanese companies for the first time ever are venturing into the tricky world of downsizing. While it is causing huge dislocations in the economy—unemployment is an unofficial 7 or 8 per cent—and even bigger dislocations for the Japanese cradle-to-grave society, the good news is the corporations that drive the country are becoming more vigorous. Despite government pressure to go slow, or not at all, with downsizing, the will is there to do it in order to gain better productivity.

You should invest in companies that make the best efforts to adjust to this competition.

The financial industry is still plagued by huge problems with non-performing loans after stock and real estate values crashed in the early 1990s. However, people underestimate the strength of the Japanese banks. Despite the tremendous losses they've taken and will continue to take (similar to American banks on LDCs and real estate), the strength of the Japanese banks is still colossal. Nine out of ten of the world's largest banks are Japanese. The merger of Bank of Tokyo and Mitsubishi Bank creates the largest banking entity in the world— greater than all Canadian banks combined. The sheer force of the Japanese banks enables Japan to engineer a reorganization of the system. The weak ones will be absorbed; the remaining banks will achieve even greater economies of size and they will rationalize their operations and emerge even stronger.

With the broader economy looking up, Japan's overall economic prospects are looking better than they have at any time over the past six years. Capital spending is strong. Profits have been surging; overall, they rocketed up 99 per cent for fiscal year (ending March 31) 1996 and are expected to climb 4 per cent during the current fiscal year. During the first quarter of 1996, Japan's economy roared ahead at an annualized rate of 12.7 per cent, the highest level in two decades. Interest rates, which are minuscule in Japan for reasons I have already discussed, have also contributed to the recovery of Japanese companies as they reschedule and refinance.

As a result, the Nikkei probably will see the 25000 level by the end of 1997. That would put it about 15 per cent higher than levels at mid-1996.

But even if the stock market ends only 10 per cent higher, I believe some of Japan's individual issues will probably rise by 20 or 30 per cent. Consumer stocks and blue-chips are recording strong profit growth and greatly benefiting from the depreciated yen.

Of course, Japanese blue-chips will be hurt along with everything else when Wall Street crashes. But if past events are any indication, the Nikkei will probably fall less than the Dow, and recover more quickly.

While the bear is about to amble onto North American equity markets, it has just finished with other markets on this continent. The bear that vanquished gold and silver has lasted sixteen years. Most commodities have gone through a prolonged slump since 1980—certainly oil and gas and food have been going nowhere. That is, until this past year, when prices took off.

I believe with the world economy strengthening and demand from the Far East, Eastern Europe, and South America (in addition to North America) increasing, commodity markets are set to recover and rise. It is possible that agricultural products—fertilizer, seeds, meatpacking— are at the start of a long-term up cycle because of worldwide demand, particularly from China and Europe. I see upward pressure on food prices (such as grains) over the next three years. Some, maybe most, of this has already been taken into account in prices of commodities and agriculture-related stocks.

As for the energy sector, oil and gas stocks will continue to benefit from increasing demand. Consider this: 40 per cent of new vehicle sales are in the gas-guzzling categories of minivan, sport utility, and light trucks. Global oil inventories are modest, and the re-entry in 1996 of Iraq into the market has made very little difference to supply.

I'm very committed to oil—both the big integrateds and some of the juniors. I think oil prices peaked temporarily at $24–$25 and we will see a weakening in price, which will impact on the companies. That weakness is the time to accumulate shares. And the more the market declines, the more reason to buy rather than sell them.

Investors can participate in commodity-price increases either through direct purchases or through stock in companies such as Noranda and Alcan. Major producers of oil, such as Royal Dutch Shell, and of fertilizer, such as Saskatchewan Potash, together with other cyclicals, will do extremely well vis-à-vis the rest of the market, and particularly well during the first decline of the overall market for blue-chip stocks. Already investors have been shifting funds from blue-chips and the general market into cyclicals.

Gold and gold stocks are a favourite of many investment advisers in a bearish market. The standard line is that they are a reliable store of value. Some firms, such as Morgan Stanley, expect the gold price to rise to $450(US) an ounce from the trading range it was stuck in during much of 1996. Certainly, gold traditionally does well in the first few months of a bear market as investors become nervous about the prospect of inflation and rising interest rates. In six of the seven sharpest stock market declines since 1987, gold stocks outperformed the S&P 500 indexes by an average 12.4 per cent.

Gold is a commodity market where the supply–demand relationship is extremely favourable. The world demand for gold exceeds the world supply from production. There are no major facilities coming on the scene; South African gold output is declining, and political risks could result in the interruption of shipments. Meanwhile, Russian output has declined significantly and its reserves are exhausted. New mining production in Russia is not likely to increase in the near future. The continuous unknown factor, however, is the action of the central banks, which have a nasty habit of flooding the market with gold sales at inopportune times (for investors).

I don't think I'd put more than 10 per cent of a portfolio in gold— bullion and stock. At one time I personally had 40 per cent of my holdings in the metal. But gold stocks have already discounted a rise in the price of the metal to $500 at a time when gold has difficulty getting past $400.

Now, I believe silver has more upside potential. For the next year or two, I believe gold will be stuck in a trading range until inflationary pressures become more apparent. With the central banks and the International Monetary Fund determined to reduce their holdings in gold, increased demand for the metal from the Far East is absorbed by such supply. Silver, on the other hand, has no central-bank competition. World inventories are reduced significantly, and silver has declined in price to such a large degree, from $50 to the current $5.30, that the upside potential in percentage terms is rosier. If you are very adventurous, you could buy silver options on the commodities exchange.

One final note about equities in the short term: There will be opportunities to own stocks in certain industries and in certain companies that will not be as adversely affected by the bear. Stocks offering biotechnology breakthroughs, for example, or telecommunications are a good bet. If you can buy these at a low price and a reasonable multiple, you should take the opportunity.

What am I personally betting on for the future? Real estate.

Property is subject to a sixty-year rising cycle, usually followed by a ten-year downturn. The current cycle probably peaked in the late 1980s and is currently still declining. It will likely reach bottom in the next two to three years.

Of course, real estate cannot be considered as a single entity. Its prospects vary according to its use and, naturally, its location. Demographics are vastly different on the West Coast and the East Coast, in Florida and in Arizona.

The key is to find a niche. An example: The market for office buildings in Canada is oversaturated, but there is healthy demand for condominiums created from converted downtown office buildings. That's what I did with a property in downtown Toronto last year and it proved a profitable venture.

Another example: Immigration is creating and maintaining a buoyant residential demand in some cities, such as Vancouver and Toronto. North of Toronto, where I live, undeveloped land has been going for a song because of the massive property bust of the early 1990s. This is an area preferred by new immigrants, especially those from Hong Kong. With some partners, I am slowly developing projects catering to that market.

Office buildings virtually everywhere are overbuilt. I doubt new office towers will be changing the landscape of North America for a very long time. However, it is a different story in South East Asia and South America. There, the landscape is changing almost week by week.

Similarly, while the demand for regional shopping centres is nil in North America and they have become very unprofitable investments, in South East Asia and Eastern Europe they are only now being built to meet a burgeoning demand. Individual investors can participate through syndicated funds such as J.P. Morgan's real estate fund.

The Next Bull

The rule of thumb in the stock market is: bear markets usually run about one-third of the preceding bull market. That doesn't mean I am calling for a seven-year bear. The corrections that have occurred along the way, such as 1987 and 1990, and even the lacklustre year of 1994, have all helped to release some of the pressure that's been building since 1982. That said, the bad news is that the other rule of thumb is: the greater the bull, the greater the subsequent bear. This has been one of the greatest bull markets in history. The Dow in August 1982 was 777; in early March 1997 it was above 7000. The coming bear will probably wipe out as much as half of the Dow, which would bring it down to 3500, or as "little" as one-third, which would bring it down to 4700. It could take anywhere from six months to three years to accomplish this devastation. Not only that, you cannot expect an immediate market recovery after such a major market meltdown. It will take some additional time and suffering before investors again venture into the stock market.

Hope springs eternal, and eventually all bear markets turn around. But while optimism is fine and good, be careful not to be naive.

The bear will reign until all those who cling to the hope that the market decline is temporary lose faith. When the financial news moves off the front page and when everybody you know who owns stocks is out of the market, that is when you can start to think about venturing back in.

The big money will be made after the débâcle, on the way up. Remember, the greatest advance is made early on (which is why you should not try to make 5 or 10 per cent by coming in at the top or by staying in at the top).

There is one requirement for success when the next bull starts his run: cool, unemotional patience. Just as you can never expect to sell at the top, you can not expect to buy at the bottom. Don't try to rush in and bottom-fish because you don't know where the bottom is. Most people make the mistake of assuming a bear market is over before it is even halfway along.

Remember, you can't count on being lucky all the time, so have a game plan. At this point, it is difficult to decisively conclude that inflation is the more likely threat to the market in the future. There are some indications that the North American economy could slide into deflation very easily. So it is imperative that you have a game plan for either scenario to enable you to act at the first sign.

If you are wrong, be willing to take small losses to prevent taking big ones. My guiding credo is: I'd rather be wrong on three or four small amounts than be hurt badly on one.

How will you know when the bear is losing his viciousness? Look for indications that sanity has been restored to the following valuations:

1. The dividend rate on the Standard & Poor's 500 should be higher than 3.4 per cent. The ideal is 6 per cent, but this is not an iron-clad rule. Much will depend on prevailing interest rates. Under certain circumstances, even a 4 to 4.8 per cent payout is okay.
   At the bottom of the bear in 1942, dividend yields were 8 per cent, while interest rates on long-term bonds were 2 per cent. The reason: The market had to convince people to buy stocks again, so frightened were they after the crash of 1929–32.
2. Book value to stock price in inflationary times is not very meaningful. In early 1997 the market had a 5-times book value. Look for something in the range of 2.5.
3. Price-to-earnings ratios have been out of this world recently. The P/E ratio on the S&P 500 is 21 times trailing in early 1997. This will come down dramatically—and not only because prices will crash. Earnings have to flatten out eventually, as a result of the coming higher-cost environment. But, as well, there is a major sea change occurring in the way North Americans view corporate earnings,

because of the widespread economic devastation caused by downsizing and cost-cutting. It has not gone unnoticed that executive compensation has shot up into the cosmos along with earnings while, at the same time, compensation to the labour force remains unchanged. I believe this trend will change as workers and politicians—rightly or wrongly—exert significant pressure to boost wages at the expense of earnings. At the end of the bear, the S&P 500's P/E ratio could be 15 times.

The August 13, 1979, edition of *Business Week* ran a lengthy feature story headlined "The Death of Equities." The magazine's timing couldn't have been better, because it neatly, although inadvertently, marked the start of the next bull market. It made sense that *Business Week* believed that stock buying was dead. It was reporting that which popular opinion deemed the truth. The bear market that most historians believe began in 1969 and turned sharply worse in 1973 had turned off shareholders by the millions—particularly younger ones who had never known a big bear. In the United States, seven million stockholders left the market during the 1970s. The playing field was left largely to the institutions. And even they despaired. In July 1979 regulations governing what pension funds could invest in—essentially, what was deemed a prudent investment—were relaxed to include not only equities and high-grade bonds, but also shares in small companies, real estate, commodities, and even gold and diamonds. At the time, market watchers sagely predicted a flight from stocks.

At the end of a bear, popular opinion always makes the mistake of declaring that stock prices will never rise again. That is precisely the time to begin thinking stocks. The *Business Week* article contained this prize declaration, which at the time should have served as an excellent buy signal: "For investors, however, low stock prices remain a disincentive to buy." Next time you read such a thing: Buy.

CHAPTER SEVEN

Crystal Ball

*"The ideas of economists and political philosophers, both
when they are right and when they are wrong, are more
powerful than is commonly understood. Indeed, the
world is ruled by little else."*

—JOHN MAYNARD KEYNES

A crystal ball gets hazier and hazier the farther out you look. The
best you can expect to do is assess risks and make educated
guesses on the direction of things. An investor can look at his
or her expectations and make sure that the rates of return he or she is
expecting are commensurate with the risk. Whenever rates of return
are exceptionally high, there's always a good reason. That's true whether
you're attracted to a financial institution offering an interest rate on
deposits way above its competitors, or whether you're piling your
money into mutual funds for the first time because of the fantastic
returns advertised for the previous few quarters or years.

Assessing risk is something I do all the time in my trading. The primary rule of thumb is that risks are proportionate to reward. But there
are different types of risks: political risk, economic risk, market risk.
The risk that our planet will collide with another one affects the survival of the human race. The probability of it happening in our lifetime is negligible. The probability of it happening over the next million
years is high—but most people are concerned with their own lifetime.

International politics is a particular interest of mine, so I'll use that as an example. The leadership situation in Russia is difficult to predict, but new developments can have unexpected consequences on the stock markets in North America and world currency markets, affecting our economy and inflation rates far beyond the imagination of the average reader of financial news. There are several possibilities: the status quo continues; or the communists retake control, in which case there are two further alternatives. One, they take power and carry out their program. Or, two, the military prevents them from assuming power, and civil war possibly erupts.

The outcome that benefits the West is obviously the status quo, a democratically elected, moderate leader. But what would be the result of a communist victory? Or a military takeover to prevent a communist restoration? Possibly the military would assume a much greater role and the market economy would be put on the back burner. Probably there would be rearmament as attempts are made to reunite the ex–Soviet Union by peaceful economic or military means. Possibly there would be a much more anti-West foreign policy. All of this of course has implications for the United States and Germany—the latter would face a weakening of the Deutschemark as the risk for their neighbours became greater.

For the United States, the impact would be mixed. The dollar would strengthen. The threat of inflation would reappear as defence spending increased. Prices of defence-industry stocks would move up. Bond and stock markets would go down.

Beyond political risks, there are localized risks. Consider the Far East: China and Hong Kong and Taiwan. If China makes threats of aggression, they have great impact on surrounding countries and markets. They can be beneficial, for example, to Toronto and Vancouver real estate markets, where immigration can lift demand, and obviously can be very positive for defence industries.

Other risks, which have nothing to do with geography and politics, can have a great impact, for example, newly emerging technologies or new products. The very rapid change in current technology, whether it is the replacement of large-frame computers by PCs—which almost destroyed IBM—or the development of the capability of small computers—which opened the door to small companies that became market behemoths, such as Microsoft, Intel, and others.

The faster the degree of change, the greater the risk and the greater the reward. When you have the emergence of winning products, there is a rapid elimination of values from their unsuccessful competitors.

How can we measure the impact of the market as a whole as distinct from individual stocks?

Three factors should be taken into account in assessing the market's zeitgeist—the three M's: Mood, Money, and Momentum.

"Mood" has been the subject of much of the discussion about the stock market in the past year or so. How are people feeling? Bullish or bearish? It's important not just for psychological reasons, but also for practical ones. The more people there are feeling bullish, the greater the danger that almost everyone who wants to buy stocks has already bought, and therefore there are no new buyers left.

"Money" is self-evident. It's the liquidity that keeps the market up. An evaporation of liquidity for whatever reason is always the reason for a bear market. A major source of liquidity for this bull has been the conversion of people's savings—not new savings—into mutual funds. Eventually that money will be used up.

"Momentum" is the measurement of how much effort is needed to keep the market moving. In the early stages of a bull market, relatively small amounts of money can move the market a relatively high percentage. At the mature stage, much more money coming into the market is required to effect change.

At the present time, there are still more and more people entering the equity markets, and there continue to be more and more mutual funds setting up shop than in the history of mutual funds. Even with all that money, the market is moving at an admittedly tremendous, but reduced, rate.

The name of the game in a bear market is to restore money to its rightful owners. This aphorism of the market refers to the phenomenon of investors of less and less sophistication getting into the market at the end—when there's less to gain. These people are pursuing reward regardless of risk, and often at this point you see new instruments introduced to the marketplace to exploit that tendency. The more of these things that are introduced, the more people get used to them, and the more they forget about the risks they are taking.

It would be wrong of me to leave you with a totally negative impression of mutual funds. I believe 99 per cent of people should be in the market by way of mutual funds. In particular, mutual funds are the only practical way an individual can be involved in global investing. And just because there is a market break in North America doesn't preclude investing in other places. Japan, for example, has already had its 60 per cent drop and is unlikely to have another.

But don't assume that mutual funds are there to protect your money. They simply allow you to participate in the market on a diversified basis. Generally, the best you can hope for from your funds is a return equal to the index. That's because the fund manager needs to keep a portion in cash reserves (where presumably it won't be making as high a return as the stock market) and, of course, there are management fees.

The other thing to mention regarding the current embrace of mutual funds by this generation of investors is that, not so long from now, the very demographics that have propelled the Dow into 7000 territory will also put an end to the party. The year 2015 is a magic one because the tail-end of the boomers will be heading into their fifties— and they will be the last to still be enthusiastically buying stocks. From there on, it's downhill as supply outstrips demand for the first time in anybody's memory. In 2015 the first wave of the baby-boomers will be busy selling their mutual funds to finance their retirement lifestyles. Meanwhile, managers of company pension funds will be doing the very same in order to make the monthly pension cheques for retired employees.

The problem is: Who will be there to buy those stocks? The children of the baby-boomers are far fewer in number and far poorer. If you want an idea of how the stock market will look then, take a look at the housing market now.

Demography has driven the historic shift in personal savings away from housing and into stocks. More personal wealth is now in stocks than houses and, indeed, in the United States, a third of American housing units are owned by persons age sixty-two and older. For the next twenty or so years, there will be no net demand for homes.

Surveys have revealed that there are actually some people who believe that their mutual funds are guaranteed, insured investments. Nothing could be farther from the truth. In fact, the only guarantee is that stock markets go down as well as up. When they do go down, don't expect that a fund will take you out of the market. You have to tell the fund company if you want to move your money out of the stock market.

There is one central point I have to make regarding bond funds and all of this talk about the death of inflation. Certainly there isn't the dire danger that it will come back tomorrow. But inflation is in the economy now—in gasoline, heating oil, medical costs, tuition fees—and therefore long-term bond funds can be just as dangerous as equity funds, particularly when interest rates are very low. Temporary money should be in short-term, five-year government bonds or Triple-A corporate bonds, waiting for the opportunity to start accumulating equity funds in the bear market. There is one caveat to this: Once it is apparent that deflation is the next danger, high-quality long-term bonds are the preferred investment vehicle.

Just how are the stock market and the economy linked? Share prices are based on investors' expectations of companies' profits. A rising market usually speaks of rosy future economic prospects. The Crash of '87 seemed to suggest they weren't linked: Growth in the United States averaged 3.5 per cent for the four quarters following the crash. However, a recession—severe in Canada because of the imposition of free trade, which resulted in huge job losses, and the country's heavy deficit burden—did arrive in 1989–90.

The risk for the next crash in North America is that the economy could follow as it did in Japan. The Nikkei plunged 60 per cent in less than three years, but the country is still paying a very heavy price economically and financially seven years later.

When a market turns, the low debt load, rising sales, widening market share, buoyant sector activity, favourable customer demographics, and brilliant corporate leadership make no difference. Obviously, if companies are already at risk because of high debt, overvalued investments (such as real estate), or rash bank loans (as in the late 1980s), a stock market crash exacerbates those problems and can cripple the economy. If the next bear market holds to the historic pattern and is followed by an economic downturn, it could be a severe one, and it could send shockwaves around the world, depressing other economies as well.

This bull market, when it comes crashing down, may pose a whole new threat to the economy. With such a significant percentage of American and Canadian households owning shares directly or through mutual funds or pension funds, the coming bear will wipe out the wealth of a far broader segment of the population than any previous crash. That will devastate not only retirement savings, but also consumer spending. Indeed, the real question for us is what will happen to the $4 trillion invested in the stock market? If people cash in and start to spend some of it (keeping most of it safe and ready for the next bull market), we will have a consumer boom. I always say, it is better to spend your money than to lose it. But another way of looking at this is: There are others things to invest in than just stocks and bonds. Buy a vineyard or put money into your children's business. These sorts of things are investments, but they help the real economy, too.

There is no doubt in my mind that the U.S. economy is strong. Indeed, stocks aren't the only things to have huge run-ups this year. Commodity inventories have been low, and commodity prices have mainly fallen or dragged sideways since the early 1980s. Demand for commodities has been strong and rising. Prices for oil, gasoline, corn, and grains rose last year. The Commodity Research Bureau Index hit an eight-year high in 1996. Trading in wheat was so great last spring that it drove the price to a record high—prompting the U.S. Secretary of Agriculture to warn that this was not a time to panic.

Commodity inflation tends to be temporary—or at least far more temporary than wage inflation. (Indeed, in 1997 oil has dropped back 10 per cent.) As well, materials make up a smaller portion of production costs than labour. Wage inflation is the real danger to the stock market.

I believe pressure on wages is building somewhat, though the realities of global competitiveness will work against too much of a run-up.

Although the case for inflation isn't so clear-cut in North America, in other parts of the world—particularly the developing world—boom times are pushing up prices significantly.

From the early 1980s to the early 1990s, financial assets have handily outperformed real assets. But over late 1995 and into 1996, the Goldman Sachs Commodity Index has beaten not only bonds and Treasury bills, but even the stock market.

Oil prices could very well stay high. Raw materials for industry—metals, plastics, paper—could move much higher if the economic recovery under way continues unabated. There are some observers, James Grant, editor of *Grant's Interest Rate Observer*, for one, who believe that because the brain trust in the economics departments on Wall Street (and Bay Street, for that matter) have ruled out inflation, it probably is just around the corner.

Anyone younger than sixty in Canada or the United States has known principally one economic condition: inflation. Since the 1970s, stocks and bonds have behaved remarkably similarly. In the market of the 1990s, both stocks and bonds sell off on good economic news. The overriding concern for both is the future of interest rates. That is the legacy of the high inflation of the 1980s. Fear of inflation rules the minds of investors, just as, in the 1940s, fear of deflation affected people's way of thinking.

A market newsletter sage a while back joked: "I can just imagine a young MBA student observing that if the stock market is up 50% in the past 18 months on 2% real GDP growth ... just imagine the money to be made if the economy could reach a 4% or 5% growth rate! ..."

Lower inflation directly benefits the stock market in that it is associated with lower interest rates. As with bonds, it is the move towards low inflation that is most bullish for equities because that is when the market is "rerated" and the biggest gains in profitability occur. In the past few years, much of the volatility in the stock market has come with swings in interest rates, which themselves were the result of the ebb and flow of fears about inflation returning. As these fears grow more subdued and rate swings lessen, the stock market will be driven more by earnings and economic prospects.

But that day is still a way off. Today, the economy often seems to be going in two directions, with statistics to prove a case for either overheated or lukewarm. In Canada, the inflation rate is below 2.5 per cent but unemployment continues to stick close to the 10 per cent mark. In the United States, the inflation rate is running at about 2.8 per cent, while the unemployment rate runs at 5.4 per cent.

A low-inflation environment doesn't always mean a higher stock market. Investors are suffering from an illusion where they do not see any inconsistency between expectation for low inflation and high nominal returns from financial markets. The fact that that has been true since 1982 has more to do with how low the markets were at that point, when inflation peaked. It has taken a long time for people's fears about inflation to fade, just as it has (and will) take a long time for people's fears about stocks to fade after a severe bear market.

The case for continuing large gains in bond and equity prices no longer exists, given that most of the adjustment to low inflation has been done. It's likely that investors, hooked on double-digit returns, will try to achieve them by taking more risk. This, of course, could be just the thing for a financial crisis.

There is an argument that we could be headed for a round of very harmful deflation and, to tell the truth, I became more convinced— although not entirely convinced—of this possibility earlier this year. Deflation was the demon that beset the economy in the 1930s following the market crash in 1929. Today, the industrialized world is in a situation opposite to the one of the 1970s, which bred the virulent inflation. Today, industrialized economies are sluggish and structurally weak because of demographics, fiscal tightening, debt problems, and globalization. Stimulus certainly isn't going to come from governments, because everywhere they are slashing spending to reduce debt.

Certainly Canada has balanced precariously on the edge of deflation for some time. The pressure to depress prices comes from every angle: Governments are slashing workers, disposable income is dropping, consumer confidence flounders, the appetite for consumer goods has bounced back only recently, companies have very little pricing power. Deflationary pressure can be found in other major economies as well: France, Germany, Britain, and Japan. In the United States, there are similar indicators of depressed demand, although also many signs of a heating-up economy. Intriguingly, it may be that deflation remains a possibility because of the very way that corporations have achieved their productivity gains—through layoffs, wage freezes, and the substitution of technology for workers. With no consumers, capacity soon outstrips demand. The only way to fight deflation would be with monetary policy, which would give stock markets a second life.

Investors have no experience with deflationary investing, and that could trigger a tremendous reaction in the markets. "The forces that were for decades aligned toward inflation are now aligned toward disinflation," Don Coxe told his clients in a report earlier this year. "A simultaneous trend reversal of such major proportions is likely to develop an irresistible momentum toward deflation ... The surprise to markets could be of seismic proportions if few companies show the ability to grow their top lines, and if a falling yen revives fears of trouble for the industrial [U.S.] Midwest."

Perhaps the best reason for expecting deflation is the recent action of the Federal Reserve in Washington: Interest-rate hikes this spring probably have killed any possibility of inflation. And while wages have spiked up, recent consumer price statistics do not paint an inflationary picture. There are arguments that deflation is already here but masked by an overstated Consumer Price Index (CPI) in the United States. The core (excluding volatile food and energy prices) CPI in the United States in January, February, and March 1997 is running at the lowest level since the summer of 1966.

So, in a deflationary environment investors should make their safest bet with three- to five-year bonds and bank stocks. In a deflationary world, banks face a higher credit risk but also much greater spreads between the rate at which they borrow money and the rate at which they lend it.

I confess, however, that I am not sure which way the economy will go, and so it is up to the individual to monitor the signs of inflation/deflation and have investment game plans already set to put into action when the trend is clear.

And keep in mind that inflation isn't the only trigger for interest-rate hikes. Rather it is rising and competing demand for money now going into equities, and that will be the major factor for the stock market in the future. When the U.S. economy recovers fully, there will be heavy pressure to divert money from the financial sector (including the stock market) into the real economy to buy useful things for industry such as plants, equipment, and raw materials. Global capital markets will determine interest rates in future.

I firmly believe that will be the most likely factor in the coming stock market crash, along with another liquidity crisis associated with the bond market.

Why a crash is likely:

1. There have been only two major buyers of U.S. government bonds: central banks (who buy the great bulk of all new bond issues) and hedge funds. These hedge funds are the most highly leveraged of customers; most of what they buy is of six months' to two years' maturity and that sets the course for the whole market up to thirty years. In other words, their buying had an impact on the yield curve, setting rates for bonds as long in term as thirty years. As I've already outlined, it is primarily the Japanese who are playing this game, because they want to keep the dollar high and the yen low. They are scared stiff that, if the dollar collapses, Americans won't be able to buy Japanese goods.

    It's impossible to keep this game going for ever. A bear market will likely commence when the Japanese stop buying U.S. government bonds. That's when you should sell your stocks.

2. No domestic money is going into bond markets; rather, 100 per cent of it is going into the stock market, which has provided the stock market with tremendous buying power. That money is only available until an increase in interest rates competes for money and lures it out of equities. The bond market, instead of becoming a supplier for the market and a source of strength, becomes a drain.

3. We don't have inflation, because we're able to maintain the bond market without the American government printing new money. The creation of new money is taking place in Tokyo, as the Bank of Japan reflates the country. That's why it can't last forever.

I believe that, while some things in our industrial and economic context have changed, they do not change the fundamental nature of the market. The market decline, when it comes, will be faster and shorter and, I hope, not as great as it otherwise would be.

The question remains: What's so different about this bull market? Why has it been able to go on longer and more extensively than ever before? What has changed?

Our understanding of economic and stock market behaviour comes largely from experience under the two philosophies that governed the Western world for this century—Marxist and Keynesian theory. Both of these philosophies had as their central core an identical message: Without a very powerful state, you cannot carry out management of the economy.

Both are now destroyed. I don't have to talk about who destroyed Marxism and how that doctrine has fallen apart around the world, even in China.

Economic liberalism of the nineteenth century was first challenged by Marxism, then shortly after by John Maynard Keynes in his seminal work *General Theory*. Following the Second World War and the economic destruction it caused, most Western governments adopted Keynesian-style policies. The central idea was an attractive one: Government, through fiscal and monetary policies, could prevent depressions and inflationary spirals by smoothing out the highs and lows of the economic cycle. That would keep the population happy enough to avoid serious social revolution. Even such a capitalistic state as the United States employed some socialism—bringing government intervention into health, unemployment insurance, safety regulation, labour laws, and old age security.

But Keynesian philosophy was destroyed by the revolution wrought by Britain's hard-line right-wing leader Margaret Thatcher and

America's Ronald Reagan. Together, they ushered in a new age of capitalism and put an end to the era of inflation. The most vital aspect of this was the freeing-up of the fundamental strengths of capitalism, which had been virtually prohibited for the previous fifty years. Even Canada became a part of this, late in the game though it was.

We experienced creative destruction, a concept first introduced by the economist Joseph Schumpeter. He had argued that capitalism was the world's greatest engine of wealth creation and, functioning freely and fully, it produced continual renewal and improvement—creative destruction. Ideally, business would be forever knocking down what it had and seeking new technologies, new methods of production and distribution, new markets to achieve a higher level of competitiveness. Schumpeter, whose ideas Thatcher seized for her own, argued that hobbling business with regulation and intervention was not only "wrong," but harmful to prosperity.

The result of the revolution unleashed by Thatcher and Reagan was indeed creative destruction. Old industries were replaced by the new. Old agricultural methods were destroyed. In its most classical sense, creative destruction has been experienced in the United States where, since 1980, 42 million jobs have been destroyed though downsizing, mergers, and productivity gains. If someone had told you that 42 million jobs could be lost, you would have expected social unrest, revolution, destruction of the market—in short, total chaos. But what happened instead was that, as whole industries shut down and companies made cutbacks, rationalizations, reorganizations, outsourcing, and the ubiquitous utilization of computers, 67 million new jobs were created. These are completely different jobs. Some are not as good—McJobs, not steel-mill jobs. Some are in industries which previously didn't exist, such as biotechnology. Some are in the same industries, but are new entities. AT&T lost workers, but Sprint picked them up. Whole new areas grew up: not just Silicon Valley and Ottawa, but also in Chicago, Boston, and Montreal.

The corporate revolution in North America began as a response to a lack of competitiveness with Japan and Germany. It began coincidentally with the start of the bull market. Nobel Prize–winning economists Franco Modigliani and Merton Miller have proposed that the rise in stock prices in the recent years reflects the present level of earnings and has just begun to reflect the rate of growth of earnings in the era of unfettered capitalism. Profit growth in recent years has accelerated to 20 per cent a year in the United States, up from an average rate of about 15 per cent earlier in the bull market.

This helps to explain how the culture of equities has grabbed such a hold on the general population. Certainly, the fallout from large corporations ridding themselves of so many employees and sending them off to be outsourcers has created millions of new entrepreneurs, often remunerated with stock options. Suddenly the market was personally important to them. And, perhaps for the first time, intelligible to them.

This also helps to explain how the bears who have been knocked down repeatedly in recent years by the climbing Dow could be wrong, and how millions of unsophisticated first-time investors, filled with blind faith and common greed, could be so right. So far.

The "purer" form of capitalism presiding in the United States, and to a much lesser degree in Canada, may possibly be a new reality in which the role of the private sector is expanded, taxes and regulations are cut, and government confines itself to guarding against inflation and defending the national currency.

If so, perhaps valuation of stocks must be reformulated. Perhaps the world *is* different.

But I believe this trend does not eliminate the business cycle—the ups and downs of the economy, the natural forces in the market—although it will likely have an impact on the bear market by making it milder and shorter.

This new reality may also create a springboard for a new bull market to later emerge, stronger and better than ever.

The re-election in November 1996 of Bill Clinton for another presidential term and the Republican-controlled Congress gave the bull a final reprieve. The election result was a dream scenario for the stock market, and it showed when the Dow responded by soaring 97 points the following day to a then-record 6177.71.

Why? Because, as one market strategist in New York was quoted as saying: "People are quite happy with divided government because it means they can't get much done. Thomas Jefferson said the less government the better, and of course that's what capitalism is all about." So the "new reality" continues.

From the buoyant perspective of early 1997, it is easier for most people to believe a recession could be in the offing rather than a major market correction.

The common assumption is that recessions are triggered by a run-up in interest rates, which then chokes off economic growth. But some argue that recessions are caused by excessive credit expansion. Austrian economist Ludwig von Mises made the case eighty-five years ago that recessions and depressions were always triggered this way. American economist Murray Rothgard convincingly argues that the Depression of the 1930s was the result, not of the 1929 stock market crash, not of a tightening of the money supply, and not of a protectionist tariff imposed at the time, known as the Smoot–Hawley Tariff—as many have argued—but rather of an exacerbated recession caused by the overexpansion of credit in the Roaring '20s.

Too much debt, too fast. This time, while business has pared down debt and built up equity, consumers have taken on record amounts of debt. In the United States, consumer credit has shot up 50 per cent from 1992 to 1996, while the economy grew by 12 per cent. Total consumer credit stood at $1.2 trillion—four times the amount they are saving each year. The trend is the same in Canada, where consumers were in hock for $129 billion at the end of 1996, which was 7.3 per cent more than the previous year. (Which, in turn, was 6.5 per cent higher than 1994.) Since 1992, the savings rate of Canadians has plummeted, while consumer credit has skyrocketed—again, to four times the rate of savings.

What does this have to do with the stock market? Two things: The mania for borrowing extends to investments, and the practice of buying shares on loan is at a record high level. Ludwig von Mises showed that the time to start worrying about recession is when everyone is beginning to feel positively euphoric.

Even a 20 per cent decline in the stock market could be followed by a nasty recession. It would wipe out at a minimum $1.6 trillion in capitalization and, with it, a big chunk of the life savings of baby-boomers-plus. The effect on the economy is impossible to calculate because recession has never occurred on such a large scale. But you can be sure those frantic baby-boomers would be rebuilding their savings, not spending on the good life and not rushing back into the stock market.

But I believe that, in the long term, the North American economy is in good shape.

The global economic trend is towards explosive growth in demand for North American goods and services. This is the direct result of the tremendous productivity gains achieved by North American industry and by the triumph of capitalism over communism, which will create up to 3 billion new consumers by the turn of the century.

The Bank Credit Analyst put it nicely when it observed that people are always underestimating the vigour and resilience of the U.S. economy. The *BCA* is predicting that that powerhouse economy is on a long-term upwave over the next five to ten years, reaping the rewards of a 3 per cent inflation environment that's here to stay. Probably.

I am convinced it is Main Street's day in the sun, not Wall Street's or Bay Street's.

As economies pull out of their tailspins, liquidity will drain from financial markets into goods and services. Eventually, North American economies will need the capital currently flowing into financial markets. Eventually, Japan will need the capital it has tied up in North American bond markets. Either way, or both, it spells crisis for North American equities markets. As that liquidity moves into economic expansion, erratic and ultimately negative capital markets will emerge.

It seems that inflation is beaten, the happy product of a concerted effort by central banks, ruthless corporate downsizing and restructuring, and Japanese deflation. But the certainty in so many people's minds that it *is* beaten causes me some worry. Inflationary pressures can start and can snowball quite rapidly. But, regardless, the script is in place for tighter money, whether inflation bumps up or not.

Historically, the best time to build cash is when its real rate of return is the lowest; conversely, the worst time to hold cash is when its real rate of return is the highest. The market will do its best to lure you down the wrong path: After all, the hardest thing to do when GICs are paying 20 per cent (as they were in the early 1980s) is to start buying stocks. Now, with stocks flying high and GICs paying peanuts, it takes real guts to cash out. Disbelieve the glib "cash-is-trash" refrain. Remember the Wall Street saying: The Fed is your friend.

The trends fuelling the bull will eventually peter out. The productivity gains that corporations have squeezed out of technology and downsizing are not limitless. At some point they will diminish significantly, or end. Baby-boomers piling savings into the market as the clock ticks towards their retirement will eventually run out of savings to convert into equities, or will come close enough to retirement that their portfolio needs will change.

The stage is being set for a deep market decline such as we had in 1974, when market indexes fell 50 per cent and low-quality stocks fell much further.

The wild-card factor is the role of the individual investor this time out. Households have become greater risk-takers over the course of the 1990s, household debt has ballooned, mutual fund sales have exploded, but individuals are already stretched financially: Credit-card delinquencies are running at an all-time high. What would higher interest rates do to that scenario?

The current bull will need a triggering event to derail it. It is not enough to say that valuations are too high. Valuations—whether it is market capitalization as a percentage of GDP at a historic high or dividend yields at a historic low—can stay excessive for long periods of time. There are, however, some valuations that have yet to reach the boiling point. And the ratio of bond yields to stock yields is not as high as it was at the top of 1987.

Once the market is structurally vulnerable, the scene is set for a catalyst. What sort of triggering event could send this bull into a downward spiral? In 1987 it was interest rates, and I believe that will be the spark to ignite the fire this time.

What has confounded stock market watchers is a situation where growth in the economy is fast enough to keep profits rising but not so fast as to create significant inflationary pressure. No one expected that to happen. But these market watchers have their eyes fixed on the wrong picture.

By the time the secular peak is reached, there will be overwhelming optimism and the bears will have long since slunk away. A major top in the market may well come with a secular turn in interest rates.

The nightmare of a global collapse could occur in an environment much like that of today: moderate global growth with steady (and even further receding) rates of inflation. So benign and so seductive to investors. Speculation is high but will likely move even higher as more and more investors are lured into the stock market. But eventually stagnant incomes and rising debt will catch up with them and the money will stop flowing. If that coincides with a desertion of the U.S. bond market by foreigners and if it coincides with a resurgence of Main Street, the stock market will not survive the triple whammy.

It comes down to a bet, as with all things in the stock market: How much are you willing to wager that this time it really is different? To decide that, you must decide how long this prosperity binge can go on without, at the very least, pausing. Then the question becomes: Is the upside—10 or even 20 per cent—big enough for the risk?

Many people believe the bull market will last into the next century. Whether we have a major decline sooner (as I believe we will) or later, how far it goes will depend on the mass psychology of people. If people remain calm, the decline might "only" be 20 per cent. But if people panic, the meltdown could be 40 or 50 per cent. It is not something that can be predicted. What I can tell you is that, with today's interconnected currency, bond, and equity markets, no market in the world will be immune from the effects of the U.S. market tumbling, and most of all, Canada.

A Dow retreating to 3300 would still mean that stocks had risen more than fourfold from 1982. A decline to 3300 would be a retracement of slightly more than half of the 1982–97 bull market—something not only reasonable, but also consistent with history.

The watershed in a decline will be a 1000-point drop, or roughly 15 per cent. Everyone believes investors are not going to panic—or rather, everyone believes that most people won't panic if the decline is limited to 15 per cent. Below that, it is not so certain.

A drop to below 6000 points is not the end of the world—we were there only a short time ago. But if there is the slightest panic, there will be another 15 per cent drop immediately, to below 5000. That will be very fast. At that point, many people will see 5000 as a great buying opportunity and there will probably be a rapid recovery that will reclaim a third of the loss. That will be the first bear-market rally. But the market is a very cruel beast and it won't be satisfied. Once the initial buying is exhausted, the selling will resume and the Dow could very well fall to as little as 3500 points, which will be a plunge of 50 per cent from the top. That, I think, will probably be the bottom. It will be over in two years.

Assessing the future for the stock market requires not so much a crystal ball as an understanding of probabilities. It boils down to basics: You must decide what is most important to you, what you can live with, what you can't, and then assign probabilities to various components of the near-term economic and financial picture.

The downside in blissfully continuing on with the herd of stock-loving investors minted in this bull market is that, if history repeats itself once again, as it has throughout this century and in previous ones, you can lose most or all of the money made during this remarkable time. The message of this book is that you should preserve capital, not for the sake of doing so, but in order to be able to reinvest it at a level which is unthinkable today. When I began my market career in 1974, in the depths of a devastating bear, stock prices had declined 50 to 60 per cent from the heights of the late 1960s and the market was full of great values. My seed money was $250,000; I was able to make more than $20 million. It was the ideal time to start a portfolio management business. Your biggest buying opportunity of a lifetime will be the *next* bull market.

Index